Table of Contents

Security

ISA

Sipp

Bonds

Income

Business

Network Marketing

Property

Shares

Royalties

Growth

E.I.S

Small Cap Shares

Angel Investing

Speculation

What is your dream day?

Recommend Reading

Other Books By The Author

Make A Living From Property

Beginners Guide To The Share Market

29 Hours A Day

Insiders Guide To Investing In Art

Niche Marketing (coming soon in 2012)

Legal

The right of Karen Newton to be identified as Author has been asserted in accordance with the Copyright, Designs and Patent Act 1988

Acknowledgments

It has been many years since I last published a book. Getting back into the routine of writing has proven more difficult than in previous years. I would like to thank my husband and daughter for their encouragement and support without which this book would still be in the handwritten planning stages.

Preface

What This Book Covers

This book is a basic introduction to investing in 2012. It provides general information on understanding terminology in today's world along with an outline of different types of investments easily available to the novice investor.

The book encourages the development of your own business as a basis to building a successful investment portfolio. Providing you with the opportunity to become self reliant.

It is hoped that this book can be used as a stepping stone to building your knowledge base for investing. Once read, I hope it encourages you to seek more technical knowledge in the areas of particular interest to you.

Intended Market

The book is aimed at the absolute beginner to investing and starting your own business. While aimed at the British market some of the information provided is readily accessible in many countries just maybe under different names.

How The Book is Structured

This book is split into 3 sections.

Section 1 – covers the tangible skills needed to start along the path to financial freedom such as setting realistic goals and putting plans into force to achieve them. It also covers financial terminology so the reader understands the difference between an asset and liability; good and bad debt and how to work to reducing bad debt. Other terminology covered such as leverage an important tool for the super rich.

Section 2 – covers my financial pyramid and how I have built and structured my finances to provide a stable foundation and build on it. It breaks down different types of investments and businesses and provides some basic information on building your own business and investing in property, shares etc.

Section 3 – this was the hardest section for me to write as it details exactly what I did to build my wealth with step-by-step details. Anyone can choose to follow the same plan that I use or develop their own unique plan.

INTRODUCTION

Have you ever wondered why some people can easily make money while others, no matter what they do, seem to loose money with every venture they start.

I became fascinated with money as a kid and dreamt of many ways of becoming rich and the fun I could have with the wealth. I read lots and lots of biographies on people who had found success and wealth. But in those days the variety of books was very limited and they were mainly biographies of actors and singers. My main problem being I couldn't sing or act so I had to find another way to make money.

It was at this time that my father told me about compound interest but I was too young at the time to fully understand its magical power. I was around 7 years old at the time and my father had just opened my first bank account. It took until almost 25 years later in the early nineties when I read the book 'Making Money

Made Simple' by Noel Whittaker and Roger Moses that I started to see the possibilities of compound interest. I did the maths over and over again and saw the real potential of compound interest. Being in my mid thirties at the time I felt I was getting too old to give it the time it needed work the way it was described in the book. The use of compound interest was put on the back burner for a few more years.

It was in 1999, when I read 'Rich Dad, Poor Dad' that I really began to understand how it could be applied to many types of investing at any age and I could still reap the rewards no matter what my age.

I started on my journey to creating true wealth in 2000. By 2003, I was able to retire and concentrate on my investments. It is amazing during those three years the number of people who told me I couldn't do what I was doing including family and friends. When I explain to people today what my husband and I did they still don't believe it. It was good having my husband working with me. We supported one another in difficult times. We constantly came up with ways to work around systems that didn't work in our favour. When family and friends said 'you're crazy, it won't work' we told each other 'go for it'.

I continue to encourage anyone and everyone to have a go for them self but the excuses I receive are just incredible. People of thirty tell me they are too old even though I point out I was forty when I started my investment journey. Another excuse I get is I can't afford it. Well, neither could I. I used £300 on a credit card and turned it into £10 million. If I can do it so can anyone.

Persistence, focus and sheer determination will get you there. I regularly, tell people about arriving in the UK with no money following the failure of a business and the death of several family members. Staying with my step-father to begin with and then buying our first house. I worked on minimum wage and the money barely covered the mortgage and council tax. We had no television because I didn't want to spend money on a TV license let alone having to waste money on buying a television. For three years we managed without a television. We would get weekly visits from TV licensing who didn't believe anyone could go without a television. My husband and I had a sole focus to create wealth. Nothing was going to stop us doing that.

Today when someone says they don't have time I just tell them the story about the television and ask them how many hours a night they spend watching TV. If they say they don't have any money again I ask how much they spend on a television license or sky or beer or cigarettes. If you are willing to make the sacrifice then you can achieve anything you truly desire. The only person stopping your success is you.

Every person has the same number of hours in a day. It is up to you what you do with those hours. And how you make those hours work for you. Do you know that if you sleep 8 hours a day for one year you are sleeping for 4 months of the year or one third of the year? If you watch television for 4 hours a day it is equivalent to watching television for two months of the year. So between sleeping and television you have lost 6 months of the year. Rather than sitting for 2 months in front of the television I would rather spend that 2 months doing something which is of benefit to me and my family, like making money. Having the money to go out and have fun with my family. What about you?

My hope is that as you read this book you will find something that is of interest. Something you can relate to and see the possibilities of making lots of money and build incredible wealth for you and your family.

Today wealth is created by those willing to make the sacrifice and have the determination to succeed. In the last one thousand years we have moved from the industrial revolution where a few people controlled the countries wealth. We have seen big business become all powerful and employ thousands. Those same businesses have today outlived their usefulness and many are failing leaving millions unemployed with little or no hope of finding work. The only opportunity available to anyone and everyone is to build your own cottage industry. Become self-employed and start looking after you and your family.

In this book you will find many opportunities available to you to do just that. Start your own business. Build a successful business and become an investor. This is your opportunity to take control of your future and that of your family.

My hope is that you grasp it with both hands and take advantage of the limitless opportunities available. It comes down to choice and you are the only one who can make the choice for you.

Good Luck on you success, I look forward to hearing from you about your successes.

If after reading this book you still need advice or help then feel free to contact me on info@karennewton.co.uk I'm sure you will find my mentoring program very helpful.

About The Author

Born in London, Karen's parents moved to Cwmbran in South Wales when she was five years old.

At twenty one years old, Karen met and married her husband, a New Zealander, who was on a working holiday in the UK.

They spent eighteen years in New Zealand before moving to Australia and then returning to the UK for family reasons. They have been back in the UK for twelve years.

Karen's employment background started with Inland Revenue where she worked as a clerical assistant on PAYE before moving to Schedule D to specialise in taxes for self-employed.

Moving to New Zealand Karen went into banking. She worked in various positions within the bank moving to new positions through promotion. Areas covered included Accounting; Teller; International Dept; Training; Visa and Corporate Lending. Karen was an Assistant Manager when she left the bank to move into her own business.

During her time in New Zealand she was joint owner of several businesses with her husband as well as individual owner of her own businesses. The businesses included Fire Protection; Security; Electrical Contracting; Air Conditioning. She was the first female member of the Fire Protection Contractors Association and went on to become its chairman. A position she held for five years. In her own right she had a Cosmetic Company and Writing Business

Attending night classes at University in New Zealand Karen studied, Commercial Law; Accounting; Business Management and Quality Management.

Karen developed her interest in writing and wrote advertorials for a local daily newspaper; Karting articles for Motorsport NZ and Karting NZ; and numerous articles sold to various magazines.

Returning to the UK in 2000, Karen worked for a recycling consortium as Administrator; Retail Manager and Quality Manager while building her investment portfolio. Being made redundant twice she eventually retired to concentrate on managing and building her investments.

Today Karen is the owner of several businesses including Property Rentals; Solar Power; Lending; Publishing; Niche Marketing; Mentoring and Network Marketing.

Author's Comments

This is the fifth book I've published. Three of the previous books were dealing primarily with investing and the fourth book was on developing personal skills mainly time management.

In my first book 'How to Make A Living From Property' I explained how to build a property portfolio through buying rundown properties, renovating them, remortgaging each property to release tax free money and then reinvesting the money back into your investment portfolio. I went on to discuss how starting with £300 in 2001, I built a portfolio worth ten million pounds by 2007. I eventually stopped buying property following the collapse of the UK banking system (known today as the credit crunch).

The growth of the property portfolio was achieved using the principals of compounding interest and reinvesting as much as possible back into the portfolio. It was an aggressive strategy but worked well in the climate of rising house prices and easy money. It worked so well that often one property would produce sufficient profit to buy another two properties. It was so successful I was able to retire in 2003 to concentrate on building and managing my portfolio. Sadly, in todays economic climate it is more difficult to achieve this kind of growth but not impossible. I will cover more on property in this book and discuss other options available to grow and sustain a profitable property portfolio.

My second book 'Beginners Guide to the Share Market' looked at using compounding interest principals to build a substantial share portfolio. The process involved two different strategies. The first strategy was buying companies whose shares are undervalued. Waiting for the share price to double in price then selling half the shares to get back the initial investment. The profit is then reinvested back into the share market in other companies who have undervalued shares.

The second strategy was to buy high yielding dividend shares, reinvest the dividend back into more shares thereby increasing the income from the shares.

Both strategies used 'Average Pound Costing' meaning the same amount was invested each month but the number of shares purchased varied depending on the price movement. Some months you could buy more shares than other months. This type of investment strategy can be successful with a small amount of £100 per month being invested to build a substantial monthly income over a few years. When told by some people finding £100 is difficult to start with then I have suggested starting with a regular sum of money being put into a savings account each week. It could be £10, £5 or even £1. Once you have £100 transfer it to high yield dividend shares. You can start slowly and build at a pace that suits you. As you start generating income from the shares it will become easier to get £100 for your next share purchase. If your share investment has generated £10 in dividends then you only need to find £90 to come up with the next £100 investment. You will be able to save that in a shorter time than it took to fund the first £100. And so the process continues.

Say you save £10 a month and it takes you 10 months to come up with your fist £100 to buy shares. You buy some just before they go ex-dividend and a month after you purchase them you get a dividend of £10. Now you only need £90 to make up your second £100 investment. This time though you only have to save for 9 months. You now purchase your next lot of shares and you get £20 in dividends. Now you need £80 to get your third £100 investment and this time it will only take 8 months. As you can see you are starting to build momentum and the time between getting your next £100 investment gets shorter and shorter. By reinvesting your money back into shares you are compounding the interest. Eventually, you will get to a stage where you earn more in dividends than the money you were putting in. You could be generating £100 a day in dividends. All from starting slowly with £10 a month.

Book three looked at Alternative Investments and in particular investing in Art. It went through the process of finding new artists and supporting their work, acquiring paintings and benefitting from the increase in value as the artist became more recognised. The book cover featured one of my favourite paintings by Laurence Reynolds. Sadly, following a stroke in 2006, Mr Reynolds lost his ability to paint and draw. His paintings continue to adorn the walls of my home. They are always commented on and the offers I have received for the paintings far outweigh the cost paid for them. I continue to believe they will increase further in value and consider them a very worthwhile investment.

Book four was a deviation from investing and looked at Time Management skills. It was called '29 Hours A Day. By putting simple procedures into place it was possible to achieve more in a day than you previously thought. This book formed part of the Niche Marketing Business I was developing.

It is now over five years since I wrote my last book. The financial and economic outlook for the world has changed drastically. We have seen the collapse of Northern Rock Bank; Bradford and Bingley Bank; Alliance and Leicester Bank and HBOS. Other banks have been merged together and many more have received bailout funds from the government to keep them operational.

The credit crunch exposed many problems within the global banking system which still have not been dealt with efficiently or effectively. Property was blamed for causing the catastrophe in reality it was the culture of greed in banking and use of derivatives behind the collapse. Today as World Leaders fail to address the problems we see banks still taking risks and paying huge bonuses resulting in little lending where it is desperately needed. Businesses have failed as their lines of financing have disappeared or been drastically reduced. Many well known high street retailers have vanished and many more continue to be at threat of closure.

Governments who supported their banks by printing more money or borrowing more money now find themselves with severe problems as they have unsustainable debt. Austerity is the new 'buzz' word. Unfortunately, austerity is not enough to solve the underlining problems facing the world today. The one thing we have learned from this disaster is that governments don't know what to do to fix the problems and if they do know what to do they aren't prepared to take the necessary steps to sort them out.

As I edit this book in October 2011, the world is on the cusp of one of the greatest financial disasters of our lifetime. We all know about the Great Depression of the 1930's but the disaster facing us today is far greater and will have more reaching consequences than the Great Depression.

I have written this book as a starting point to help the beginner to investing to survive 2012 and beyond. Although called 'Surviving 2012' I believe the disaster facing us will last another 10 years or so. In that time the world will have totally changed from that we know today. Businesses providing the bulk of employment will have disappear and there will be some new ones in their place but on the whole I think we are moving from a dependency on finding a job to one of creating our own job.

Self-employment and home businesses will be the new growth area as a population comes to realise they can no longer depend on big business to provide jobs. They can no longer rely on the government to provide benefits. They can only rely on themselves to provide their own job and self worth. Only they can provide for their families. For that reason I have included a section on setting up your own business.

The aim of this book is to provide some ideas on finance, investing and self-employment.

A word of caution – I don't claim to have the answers to surviving the coming financial disaster. This book is just to give you some ideas, show you what I am currently investing in and how I hope I've prepared my own investments to survive the coming decade and come out stronger in the years ahead.

I believe the wealth in this country will transfer from big business to those people who are prepared to take action now and be ready to reap the rewards in the next decade. This is the starting point for you to enjoy some of those benefits.

Section 1

Skills & Knowledge

Section 1 - Introduction

Section 1 of this book covers basic financial education and investment skills. Some of it you may already know and I apologise if you feel you are going over information you already know. I hope instead of skipping sections you will take a moment to refresh yourself as some things may have changed recently.

If this is the first time you are reading any of the information please take the time to digest it and to make sure you fully understand it before moving on to the next section it could make the difference between making £100 and making £1,000,000 or even losing everything.

Knowledge is the key to unlocking your financial future and surviving 2012. Choices are the action steps to making it happen.

Fast Money

In the words of an old song 'money makes the world go round, the world go round, the world go round. Money makes the world go round, of that we are sure, on being poor.'

Have you ever paused for a moment and thought about how quickly your money moves around the UK let alone around the world. In the world of technology we are dealing with 'Fast Money'. The same pound you spend today is at the same time being spent by thousands of other people. The money has moved so fast it is instantaneously available to thousands of other people.

Example

You work for a company called Printalot. Printalot provides stationery to many businesses and government departments. One government department is called Teachmemore School.

Teachmemore places an order with Printalot for text books. The books are sent to Teachmemore along with a bill which is duly paid by Teachmemore. It's a simple transaction of the kind that takes place everyday in thousands of businesses up and down the country.

Now let's look at the flow of money.

Teachmemore ⟶ Printalot

But look at the circle of money movement which allows Teachmemore to be able to pay Printalot. The money starts with Printalot paying your wages out of which your taxes are paid to the government. The government then uses tax payer's money to set up government departments such as Teachmemore who in turn spend money with Printalot. The diagram below shows the flow of money.

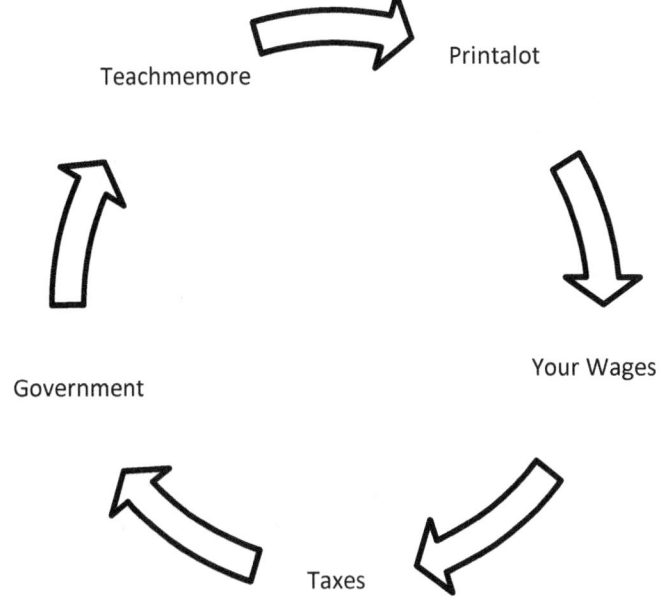

Teachmemore

Printalot

Government

Your Wages

Taxes

Money is continuously moving and at great speed. So fast most people take it for granted and tend not to realise how the money is moving. Central to moving all the money around is the banks. So using the diagram above and putting in the movement between banks you can see how quickly the money is starting to move.

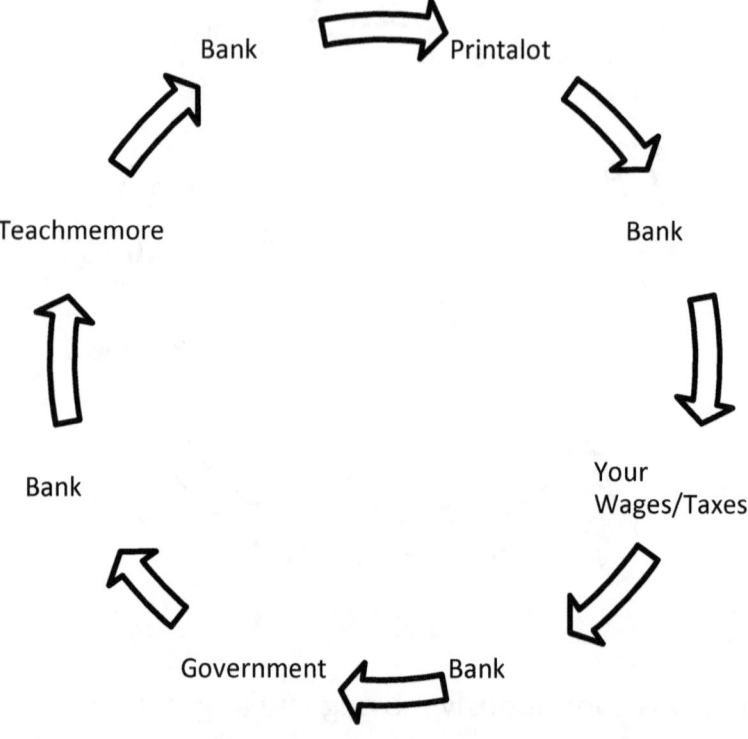

In every transaction it is not physical money that is moving it is a promise from each participant in the transaction that the money will be there to cover the payment. Confidence between each party that the money will be available allows the transactions to take place.

What happens when there is a loss of confidence?

In 2007 the Northern Rock Bank was hit by a lack of confidence and the rumour mill started that Northern Rock had run out of money. I'm sure you all remember the pictures of queues of people outside every branch of Northern Rock. People panicked and wanted to get their money from the bank.

The lack of confidence continued and soon banks stopped doing business with one and other. The flow of money slowed down and gradually ground to a halt. By February 2008 nobody was prepared to do business with anyone else in the banking arena. This became known as the credit crunch. It wasn't just isolated to British banks. As a global industry, what affected a bank in America had repercussions on a bank in India. What happened in UK affected banks in every part of the world. The confidence between banks ran out and money stopped flowing. The world ground to a halt.

How to get money moving again?

Governments around the world decided the best way to restore confidence to the financial world was to become the guarantor and lender of last resort for the banks. Governments started the printing presses making more and more money and giving it to the banks to make sure they had money and attempt to restore confidence into the banking system.

The lack of confidence ultimately caused the worst recession the world has seen in a generation. There were other factors contributing to the problems but this is a simplified view of the problem to help you understand what effect the global financial world has on your everyday life.

Laws of Physics

The laws of physics state that for every action there is a reaction.

So let's move forward to 2011. Governments around the world have been so busy printing money to bailout the banks they have created enormous debts which simply put, they can't afford.

The new 'buzz' words are austerity measures. Governments worldwide are reigning in their spending, reducing the level of debt they hold and trying and get back to the levels of debt which are more realistic for each country. And so another cycle has started. The whole world is again grinding to a halt. Money in circulation is being reduced and confidence among banks is looking shaky again. The level of confidence between banks can be seen quickly by watching the LIBOR rate. Over the past year it has risen to 1%. It might not seem much but considering Bank of England has kept rates at a record low of 0.5% it is a concern to see banks inter lending rates increasing at a steady pace. This time governments are broke and don't have the money to pump into the ailing banks. The future is looking very bleak.

Governments who borrowed money to pump into the banks are struggling to meet their loan repayments. We have all heard about Ireland, Portugal, Italy, Greece and Spain who have major financial problems and have had to receive bailouts from the IMF (International Monetary Fund) and the emergency fund set up by Europe called EFSF. These countries (and there are more waiting in the wings) are likely to bring down Europe and the Euro along with peripheral countries. The world is heading into a depression the likes of which has never before been seen.

What I have described is only a sample of the world's economic woes. If you want to understand more about the banking system or world economies there are numerous books around which will give you more in depth information.

Eye of the Storm

In the previous pages, I've given a brief overview of the problems we are facing. I've also been trying to make you aware of the financial storm heading our way. From 2009 – 2011 we have been in the eye of the storm. Anyone who knows anything about storms or hurricanes knows that the second part of the storm is usually worse than the first part. We still have the second part of the storm to hit us. The impact on the world will be unimaginable in the way it will affect every single person in the world.

It will definitely be survival of the fittest. How you survive the storm will depend on how well you prepare for it. How strong your financial foundations are to stand up to the battering they will take.

We are about to see one of the greatest transfers of wealth the world has ever seen. This is your opportunity to be part of it and benefit from it. But it will only happen if you are prepared to take the action needed to survive 2012.

Why You Need To Know About Fast Money?

If you go back in history there was no money only a bartering system where each party decided on the value of the item they were selling. You might have traded 3 cows for one horse or you may have traded some wine for material to make clothes.

Later gold and silver became currency. If you bought a horse you paid by gold or silver coins. In some instances where the purchase was not worth a full silver coin or gold coin then a piece of gold or silver would be clipped off the coin as payment.

Paper became the next form of currency initially backed by gold and later backed by a promise to pay.

Today we are in the digital age and money is a cyber transaction. It moves very quickly from one transaction to the next. To survive 2012 and beyond your investments also needs to move quickly.

For instance, if you are a regular savings type putting money into a bank account paying little or no interest your money will become less and less valuable. In 12 months time due to inflation your money will buy you less and less. The interest you receive doesn't keep up with inflation your money becomes worthless. However, if you can keep your money moving quickly into new investments paying higher than inflation returns then you will become wealthier.

With any investment that I make I am looking at how quickly I can get my initial deposit back. When I was buying property, prices were rising so quickly that I could get my deposit back within 4 weeks. I still retained the property but I got my deposit back and it was then available for the next investment. I kept my money moving and had fast money. When I invest in shares for capital growth, I have a timeframe for doubling my money and releasing the initial deposit. I sell half the shares to get my money back and keep the other half. The released money is then available for the next investment.

The faster you can learn to move your money the more money you will make. It is a skill that takes time to learn but once learnt the money starts rolling in.

Good or Bad Debt

'The crisis we face is a crisis of debt' says George Osborne, Chancellor of the Exchequer and David Cameron, Prime Minister of UK. 'We are not able to borrow money to make the problems go away. That will increase the debt and make it worse. We must reduce our debt. Not just the government's debt but the debt of every single person'

Are They Right or Wrong?

Well, they are actually both right and wrong. 'How can that be?' I hear you asking.

There are two types of debt. Good Debt and Bad Debt. Good debt is money you have borrowed to purchase assets that produce income for you. Bad debt is money you have borrowed to purchase items that lose their value and entice you to spend even more.

Governments are notorious for running up bad debt. How much money does the government spend on the NHS? Money it borrows and has to pay interest on. It then gives the borrowed money to the NHS. The money disappears into the system. The government then has to borrow more money to pay off the current loan. The circle goes on and on and on and on ..... I think you get the picture. This type of debt is a bad debt.

In its defence, the government will say it is hoping that in the coming years, inflation will make the debt seem smaller and hence easier to pay. But the government has no intention of paying off the debt as it needs a continual supply to money to run the NHS. The debt gets larger and larger and we end up paying more and more in taxes to cover the cost of the loans.

Imagine a situation whereby the government charged every patient in hospital for the care they received. The government would know on average a certain amount of people sick everyday, it would know on average it had a certain amount of money coming in every day. Now the money it had borrowed would not appear to be as bad as the government knew it had a way of paying off the debt and making some profit along the way.

Now I'm not advocating the Government start charging every patient but I use this example just to show you how money is used.

Bad Debt

The sad thing about bad debt is that very few people realise they have it. If you point out to them the things they have borrowed money for that is bad debt they make excuses that it was necessary to incur that debt. Unfortunately until bad debt is identified and removed trying to get on top of your finances is going to prove very difficult.

An example of bad debt is a loan to purchase a car. A store charge card is another and a credit card used for everyday purchases is yet another example of bad debt. In almost every case the purchased item will probably not be around in five or ten years times when you are still paying off the loan. If say you bought a car for fifteen thousand and took out a loan from the bank for ten years. In ten years time it is unlikely you will still have the same car and if you did it would only be worth a few hundred pounds. Adding on interest you have probably paid in the region of thirty thousand pounds for a vehicle which is now worth on a few hundred pounds. Does it sound like a good idea to have paid out all that money and just have a rust bucket of a car left to show for your borrowed money? You now need another car and are in the vicious cycle of having to borrow again to get another car. This time due to inflation you have to borrow a larger sum of money, pay back even more and still have nothing but a rusty old car left to show for all the debt you incurred.

Good Debt

If you had borrowed fifteen thousand pounds towards purchasing a rental property which was generating income of say five hundred pounds a month. The same fifteen thousand pounds becomes a good debt. It's a good debt because after ten years you still have the property, it would still be generating an income for you and it, the property, would still have value. The same good debt can be of value as it can reduce your taxes and greatly improve your income. The surplus income can be used to lease your vehicle or purchase it.

In Rich Dad, Poor Dad by Robert Kiyosaki, Robert wrote a definition of good debt and bad debt. He says that good debt puts money in your pocket and bad debt takes money out of your pocket.

Now review the debts you have and see if you have good or bad debt. If it's good then leave it alone for now. If it is bad debt then your first task is to try and reduce it and pay it off as quickly as possible.

Paying Off Bad Debt

If you have bad debt your aim should be to get rid of it as quickly as possible. Draw up a budget that you can stick to. Work to reduce your cards, loans, overdrafts with any spare cash you have available. If you aren't any good with budgets then get some help. There are many organisations that can help you. Don't be embarrassed to ask for help. It's their job and what they are there for, to help you.

The simplest way to reduce credit cards is if you have several cards select one card and put it away where you can't get access to it. If you think you would be too tempted to use it then cut it up.

Increase the monthly payments so you pay more than the minimum. You could do this by increasing the payment by £10. More if you can afford it. Once the card has been repaid apply the same procedure to the next card. Keep doing this until all the cards have been repaid.

If you can keep the cards and not cut them up all the better as later in the book I will show you how you can turn credit card debt into good debt.

How Inflation Can Help You

Inflation is one of those horrible ailments of the modern world. We need it to keep a healthily economy but too much of it and it does terrible damage to our finances.

The Bank of England has been given the task of keeping the rate of inflation at 2% or below. This is thought to be a healthy indication of a growing economy. Unfortunately for us, as I write this the rate of inflation in the UK is 5%. It is expected to reduce in 2012 when the effects of the increase in VAT are no longer included in calculating inflation.

From an investment point of view we need to be making more money than the rate of inflation otherwise we are getting poorer not richer. As an example:

Let's say I spend £100 per year on groceries. With an inflation rate of 5% next years groceries are going to cost me £105.

If I put the same £100 into a savings account earning just 0.01% (which many of them currently do) then after a year I would have earned a total of 1 penny in interest.

As your savings have not kept up with the rate of inflation you would not be able to purchase the same amount of groceries for your money. So inflation has a negative impact on your finances.

Good Inflation

As with most things in our financial world there is a good side and a bad side. So it follows that there is good inflation and bad inflation. Above we took a quick look at bad inflation where our spending money buys us less each year as inflation increases. However, there is also a good side to inflation.

A friend of mine got married in 1987. She and her husband bought a property for £15,000.

They put down a deposit of £1000 and borrowed £14,000 as an endowment policy mortgage. The mortgage was over 25 years so in 2012 it will be repaid using the endowment policy. Today, through inflation their house bought for £15,000 is now worth £169,000. The mortgage payments of around £130 a month seemed a lot when they first bought their house but today with wage increases and inflation it is very little money being repaid each month.

Inflation has worked in the favour making the payments on their property over time seem so small.

This is the tactic that governments use all the time. They need inflation so today's debt will in the future seem to be a very small amount.

We can use the same principles to buy rental properties. If when my friends got married you had purchased 10 rental properties. And assuming they were on interest only you would still have a mortgage to repay of £140,000.

(£15,000 less £1000 deposit multiplied by 10 properties) The value of one property is £169,000. If you sold one property it would repay the mortgages on all 10 properties and you would be left with 9 properties worth £169,000 each all of them mortgage free. Your 9 properties would be worth £1.5 million pounds. (£169,000 x 9 = £1,521,000) The properties would also generate an income for you. If rented out at a modest £500 per month that equates to an income of £4,500 a month.

I use the term modest as the average rental per month is current around £700 per month.

Using this example we have used inflation to create a wealth of £1.5 million pounds. So inflation does have its good advantages.

Leverage

Leveraging allows you to own, benefit or utilise an asset as if you owned the whole asset.

Rental properties are a good example of using leveraging. You can purchase a property worth £100,000 with just a 15% deposit. (Shop around there are mortgages still available) You have put down £15,000 and used leverage of 85% to have 100% use of a property.

You now have a property that you own, control and benefit from as if you had bought the property without a mortgage. You can charge rent and the rent should cover the cost of the mortgage along with other legal compliances and you should still have sufficient left over to provide a small income.

Property is just one example of the use of leveraging. There are many products that the rich use to leverage. Gold is another use of leveraging where buyers purchase on margin.

Margin is another term for leverage. When buying Gold on Margin you put down a deposit of around 10% for the gold you are purchasing. So if you are buying £10,000 of Gold you need only pay £1,000 deposit. If Gold goes up in price you can sell the gold and pocket the profit as if you had paid the full £10,000 for the gold.

If you look around at the different assets you will find leveraging possible in property, shares, commodities and Forex just to name a few.

Buying a business provides another example in the use of leveraging. With a small down payment and a loan for the remainder good income producing ready made businesses can be found.

The rich use leveraging to its maximum ability. The only difference between them and you is their knowledge of how to gain leverage and where to use it.

Once you have that knowledge you too will start using leveraging to increase your wealth.

Other types of leverage

While this is meant to be a financial book it is worth noting that in our daily lives there are other forms of leverage which if or when applied greatly ease the way we do things.

- **Other People's Knowledge** – by reading books, magazines and articles about your chosen topic you are using the knowledge and expertise of other people to improve your understanding of the topic helping you avoid the pitfalls they experienced in gaining their knowledge.
- **Other People's Ideas** – someone may have an idea that you can capitalise on. Suppose someone has invented a system that guarantees success in selling any product wouldn't it be easier to use the system to sell your product rather than spend a lot of time developing your own system.

- **Other People's Contacts** – having the right knowledge and system moves you closer to achieving your goals. When buying buy-to-let properties I use a broker to organise the mortgages. When I first started buying property I used numerous people all claiming to be brokers unfortunately, they very rarely delivered the type of finance I needed. Someone suggested I try a particular financial broker. He has now arranged finance on over 90% of my deals. Another person's contact became my best team member in building my wealth. Who do you know who may just have the contacts you need to build your wealth?

In his book Focal Point, Brian Tracy says there are 7 types of leverage which can double your income and halve the time you spend making it.

Compound Interest

The 'magic' of compound interest has to be one of my all time favourite topics when it comes to investing and financial education.

In 1995, I purchased a book written by Noel Whittaker and Roger Moses called 'Making More Money'. Noel Whittaker and Roger Moses wrote about compounding interest in the form of a fairytale called 'The Fairy Godmother and the Magic Train'. Included with the story was a chart showing the effects of compound interest over a lifetime of regular investing and reinvesting interest? Initially, I found the figures unbelievable but after sitting down with my calculator and doing the maths on the charts it was incredible. A real eye opener on the power of compound interest.

The basis of the story is, if you save £2.73 per day equivalent to £1000 a year and put it into savings earning 14% per annum, each year you reinvest the interest, by year 6 you would be receiving more in interest per year than you are contributing. If you kept the savings going for 37 years interest earned would be £133,921 and your savings pot would be worth £1,130,221 (over a million pounds). After 37 years you could stop contributing the £1000 a year and just let the interest reinvest. By year 50 your savings pot would be worth £6.2 million and by year 60 it would be worth over £23 million. The maths is simple, take a few minutes to work it out and you will be amazed at what £2.73 per day could create for you.

Now you might understand how powerful a Junior ISA or a Childs Trust Fund could be for your children and what an excellent start in life it could provide for them. Imagine, how wealthy you would be now if your parents had saved £2.73 a day for you?

Don't think it's too late for yourself, you might not have 60 years of savings available to you but after just ten years what could you have achieved.

The principal of compound interest is to reinvest the interest earned back into the same pot and then earn interest on interest.

This principal I used which helped me turn £300 into £10,000,000 in six years with property. It's the same principal I use with shares by reinvesting the dividend and capital growth back into more shares.

You might think 14% isn't possible but work out the returns from £300 to £10 million. It is far greater than 14%. With shares I have dividends worth 17% and more. P2P lending offers high rates of return some of mine are at 13% and if reinvested they offer wonderful opportunities to make the most of compounding interest. There are more investments out there earning just as good a rate of returns. You just have to look for them.

I have to admit I get very excited about compound interest. The opportunities are endless and that is why compound interest is one of the most important tools to help you create substantial wealth.

But if you are sceptical have a look at the chart below. It's a simple chart using 5% interest per annum reinvested and contributing £1000 a year. For this exercise I haven't deducted tax. The example is to show you how effective compound interest can be.

Compound Interest Table 1

Year	Deposit	Interest	Balance	Year	Deposit	Interest	Balance
1	£1000	£50	£1050	11	£1000	£710.34	£14917.15
2	£1000	£102.50	£2152.50	12	£1000	£795.86	£16713.01
3	£1000	£157.63	£3310.13	13	£1000	£885.65	£18598.66
4	£1000	£215.51	£4525.64	14	£1000	£979.93	£20578.59
5	£1000	£276.28	£5801.92	15	£1000	£1078.93	£22657.52
6	£1000	£340.10	£7142.02	16	£1000	£1182.88	£24840.40

7	£10 00	£407 .10	£8549 .12		17	£10 00	£129 2.02	£2713 2.42
8	£10 00	£477 .46	£1002 6.58		18	£10 00	£140 6.62	£2953 9.04
9	£10 00	£551 .33	£1157 7.91		19	£10 00	£152 6.95	£3206 5.99
10	£10 00	£628 .90	£1320 6.81		20	£10 00	1653. 30	£3471 9.29

As you can see from this chart by year 15 you are earning more in interest than you are contributing each year.

Based on today's university fees if you started saving when your child is born by the time they reach university age you would have sufficient funds to pay for their tuition. What a great start in life for your child. No debt coming out of university and no worries about how they would pay their fees. And much less stress for you knowing you had the money available when you needed it.

Now if you were to extend this chart for another 20 years you can see how effective compounding interest can be.

Compound Interest Table 2

Year	Deposit	Interest	Balance	Year	Deposit	Interest	Balance
21	£1000	£17815.96	£37505.25	31	£1000	£35318.04	£742918.90
22	£1000	£19225.26	£404030.51	32	£1000	£37644.95	£790603.85
23	£1000	£20711.53	£435022.04	33	£1000	£40003.19	£840607.04
24	£1000	£22225.10	£467217.14	34	£1000	£42533.35	£893200.39
25	£1000	£23836.36	£501113.50	35	£1000	£45156.02	£948306.41
26	£1000	£25555.68	£53669.18	36	£1000	$4791.82	£100628.23
27	£1000	£27313.46	£574072.64	37	£1000	£50801.41	£1067109.64
28	£1000	£29220.13	£613202.77	38	£1000	£53855.48	£113095.12
29	£1000	£31116.14	£654378.91	39	£1000	£57044.74	£119799.86
30	£1000	£332	£6976	40	£1000	£604	£1268

	00	1.95	0.86			00	0.00	39.86

As you can see from the above tables it took 15 years before you were earning as much in interest per year as you were contributing. It only took another 8 years to double the interest amount to £2071. By year 40 you would be earning 6 times more than you are contributing to the investment pot.

Now lets extend the investment table out for another 20 years and see the accumulative effect of compound interest.

Compound Interest Table 3

Year	Deposit	Interest	Balance	Year	Deposit	Interest	Balance
41	£1000	£6392.00	£134231.86	51	£1000	£11040.78	£231856.34
42	£1000	£6761.59	£141993.45	52	£1000	£11642.82	£244499.16
43	£1000	£7149.67	£150143.12	53	£1000	£12274.96	£257774.12

44	£10 00	£755 7.16	£1587 00.28	54	£10 00	£129 38.71	£2717 12.83
45	£10 00	£798 5.01	£1676 85.29	55	£10 00	£136 35.64	£2863 48.47
46	£10 00	£843 4.26	£1771 19.55	56	£10 00	£143 67.42	£3017 15.89
47	£10 00	£890 5.98	£1870 25.53	57	£10 00	£151 35.79	£3178 51.68
48	£10 00	£940 1.28	19742 6.81	58	£10 00	£159 42.58	£3347 94.26
49	£10 00	£992 1.34	20834 8.15	59	£10 00	£167 89.71	£3525 83.97
50	£10 00	£104 67.41	£2198 15.56	60	£10 00	£176 79.20	£3712 63.17

These tables were calculated using 5% compounding interest per year. As I said earlier if the same figures were used but interest was calculated at 14% then by year 60 the balance in your account would be £23 million.

All this is achieved from saving just £19.23 per week and using the principles of compound interest getting your savings to grow.

I hope you are as excited about compound interest as I was when I first read the book by Noel Whittaker and Roger Moses. It is so easy to turn £19.23 a week into millions. With this book you will see how easy it is to use compound interest principles and grow you wealth. 14% is easily achieved when you increase your financial knowledge. There are numerous ways shown throughout this book.

Assets and Liabilities

In his book 'Rich Dad, Poor Dad' Robert Kiyosaki described an asset as something that puts money in your pocket. He described a liability as something that takes money out of your pocket. He then went on to cause a furore by saying your home is not an asset.

So let's look at his comments and see if you agree with him. If you own your own home does it have a mortgage? Who pays the mortgage? Where does the money come from to pay the mortgage, council tax, water rates, electricity and gas charges? Using Robert Kiyosaki's definition of a liability it is something that takes money out of your pocket. So is your house an asset or a liability?

Look at it from a different point of view. You own a rental property with a mortgage. You charge £500 a month to the tenant renting it. This covers the cost of paying the mortgage, paying for maintenance, paying for legal compliances and still having a little left over to give you something to go in your pocket. The tenant pays Council Tax, water rates, electricity and gas charges. This is an asset because it puts money in your pocket.

I hope you can see the difference between an asset and a liability using the above examples. Property is not the only type of asset available. I'm also not saying you should sell your home. What I am trying to do is help you understand the difference between assets and liabilities so the next time you go to buy something you ask yourself the question 'Am I buying an asset or a liability?' If you are buying an asset great, it will increase your income and this book is about increasing the income producing assets you hold. If it's a liability, I hope you will think again before buying it and wait until you have lots of assets producing lots of income and then you will be in a better position to afford the liability.

Income Producing Assets

As I stated earlier, the aim of this book is to build a portfolio of income producing assets. These are assets that produce money that keeps coming in every month whether you choose to work or not. This type of income is called residual income. It is something you will read more about later in the book.

Grab yourself a sheet of paper and make a list of all the assets you have remembering the definition of an asset as something that puts money in your pocket. To help you get started I have made a list of some of my own.

Residential Rental Property

Commercial Property

Network Marketing Business

Other business' (these are businesses that you own but don't need you working in them)

Royalties

Dividends from Shares

Other Investments

If you have a nice big list of income producing assets congratulations you don't need to read any further. I'll probably ask you to give me some advice!

If your income producing assets are low or non-existent then let me explain the list I've made above and how it can help you.

Residential Property – one of my favourite assets. You purchase a property that is let to a tenant producing an income. The rent covers your mortgage payments and other costs and you have any surplus income as your income

Commercial Property – basically the same as Residential Property except you are dealing with a business'. You still have a tenant who pays you regularly sometimes on a monthly basis and sometimes on a quarterly basis. It is still money going into your pocket.

Network Marketing – this is a business that initially requires you to do some work by building up networks of customers and other people who also want to have their own business known as distributors. You receive income from your customers and your distributors. Once you have reached a certain level the business will naturally continue growing along with your income.

Other Business – these are businesses that you own but don't have to work in on a daily basis. For example Richard Branson owns the Virgin brand. Virgin has around 300 businesses. Richard Branson cannot work in every business every day. He owns the businesses but has managers responsible for their daily running.

Richard Branson would be paid a dividend from his businesses as his income not a wage or salary. In other words he works on his business not in the business.

Royalties – if you create a song you receive a royalty every time someone buys the song, downloads it or it is played on the radio. Another example of Royalties is books where the author receives payment for every book that is sold. Are you any good with inventions? You next bright idea may just provide you with a royalty for life.

Dividends from Shares – one of the strategies previously mentioned is buying high yielding dividend shares. Some companies will pay you a dividend quarterly for every share you hold. Some companies pay twice a year and others annually. There are some companies who don't pay any dividends. But from our point of view buying high yielding dividend shares paying us a regular income is an asset.

Other Investments – some of the assets I hold under the title of 'other investments' include

Lending Portfolio where I lend money to individuals and business and receive monthly interest during the term of the loan.

Angel Investing – this is where I loan money to a start up business or a business wanting to expand. In return I get a dividend on my money, and/or a share in the company and a dividend.

Enterprise Investment Scheme (EIS) where I invest in government qualifying companies for either a potential dividend or a potential tax free capital gain.

There are many types of income producing Assets but if you stick to the above as a starting

point then you will quickly build your wealth
and your income.

Getting What You Want

If you are like me the word 'goals' is enough to send the mind into sleep mode. I've had goals rammed down my throat so much that my brain shuts off at the very thought of setting goals, monitoring them and beating myself over the head when I fail to achieve them. So for me I have a different approach.

I still have goals because without them I would never achieve anything. Whether you like goals or not if you don't have something to challenge yourself and some way of monitoring your progress then how do you know if you are improving your financial situation or making it worse?

If you join my mentoring program you will receive the tools that I use daily to monitor my progress. It's a simple way of pulling everything together financially and seeing if you are improving your income and net worth or going backwards. It takes me about 10 minutes a day and I have an up to date record always on hand.

My goals are written down and each day I work towards achieving them. But instead of getting annoyed with myself if I haven't worked on the goal or completed it I ask myself two questions.

- What have I done today to improve my income?
- What have I done today to improve my net worth?

If the answer is nothing then I don't go to bed until I have done something for each question. It might be writing a few more words for my next book which will increase my income once it's finished. It might be buying some more shares; lending more money; taking a walk around the estate agents and arranging some viewing appointments for potential properties; paying off a loan or credit card; signing up a new tenant; filing documents with the court to get rid of a bad tenant; talking to a potential new distributor or customer. There is an enormous list of things I can do each day that will eventually have an impact on improving my income and improving my net worth. Some actions are instant other may take weeks or months to have any impact but the important thing is I have taken action every single day.

In his book, The Compound Effort, Darren Hardy says that each day we make little choices that have an impact on our lives in 1 year, 5 years or 10 years. If I choose not to write the extra 1000 words today what would the impact be for the future? In all likelihood, if I put off writing those words today I will have an excuse tomorrow, the day after, next month and next year. The final result being that I probably won't finish writing the book. But if today I made the effort to write 1000 words today and another 1000 tomorrow and develop the habit of writing 1000 words everyday then my book will be written very quickly. Once the habit is in place then instead of producing a book each year I could probably produce a book twice or three times a year. What impact does that have on my income?

Why not give it a try and see how you go. Ask yourself the two questions every day. What have I done today to improve my income? What have I done today to improve my net worth?

If you are not using goals at the present then it is better than nothing. If you go full gusto and set up loads of goals and then don't follow up with them this simple approach might help you achieve your goals easier. If you are brilliant at setting and achieving your goals, well done, treat yourself to a drink at the pub tonight and then write a book about it.

Cycles

The financial world works in cycles. The best way to imagine a cycle is like a circle. At the top of the circle is the high for the investment. At the bottom of the circle is the low for the investment. The left and right hand sides of the circle tell you if are in an upward or downward cycle and helps provide a focal point of where you are. The trick to investing is getting into the investment at the bottom of the circle and getting out at the top of the circle. The problem being that no one knows when the investment is at a high or when it is at the low.

To give an example of a cycle lets look at property. I came back to the UK in 2000. At that time in my area of South Wales you could purchase a nice 3 bedroom house for £30,000. House prices were steadily rising and by 2007 the same house was selling for £115,000. Today house prices are going down and the house is worth about £90,000. Will it go back down to £30,000 unlikely but you never know.

Property Price
2007 £115,000

Property Price
2011 £90,000

Will prices
continue to drop
or will £90,000
become low for
next cycle

Property Prices
2000 £30,000

Property Prices
2004
£85,000

If you had purchased the house for £30,000 and sold for £115,000 you would be very pleased with the profit you had made. You bought at the low of the cycle and sold at the high.

The story would be totally different if you bought at the high of £115,000 and were now wanting to sell at today's price of £90,000. It would be a loss and you would not be very happy with the result. Unfortunately, this is a situation many property owners currently find themselves in at present. The value of their houses has dropped to below the price they purchased the property for and due to the size of the mortgage they have on the house they find themselves in negative equity. There are many property owners now waiting for house prices to go up so they can sell.

There are different cycles for different investments. Take Gold as another example, it is still climbing in value. If you had purchased Gold at $400 USD and it is currently at $1600 USD you would be very happy with the result. The big question is 'Has Gold reached the cycle high yet?' Nobody knows the answer to that. We all like to think we have a crystal ball and can predict the rise and falls but we don't and we just do the best we can.

I keep my own cycle information in a simple excel spread sheet. I use the information to help make a decision on whether to buy or sell. I don't base it solely on the cycle but it does help as part of my overall criteria for an investment.

Cycles can be a very handy tool but don't get hung up on them as they only tell part of the story.

Bull or Bear

If you have heard the terminology of a bull market or a bear market you are probably wondering what it means. Simply put if we are in a bull market the share market is in an upward trend. If we have a bear market it is in a downward trend. This is just a different terminology for a cycle.

Interestingly Bull markets tend to last longer than bear markets. In other words when a share market drops in value it drops very quickly. But when it grows it continues in an upward trend for a long time before going down again.

Teams

When it comes to the world of finance the people who are the most successful are the ones who can build good teams around them.

Business Teams – this is an example of a great team. When you have the right infra-structure in place you have staff running and improving your business without you being present. You have staff producing your product or providing your service. Salesmen getting work for you. Managers making the business run smoothly and profitably, administrators keeping on top of invoicing and paperwork; accountants who advise the best structures for your business and minimise your tax; solicitors who prepare contracts. Your job is to get the best team possible to run your business.

Network Marketing is also about building teams. In this instance as well as building your customer base you are building a team of people who duplicate what you do and help you to build your business.

Property – having a successful property business is also about building a great team around you. You need to have relationships with Estate Agents and people who can source property deals for you; mortgage brokers who can source the best mortgages to suit your needs; solicitors who can complete transactions within a reasonable time; tradesmen who can renovate your property within a few weeks; an accountant who can advise the best structure for your business and provide tax minimising options.

Share market – you need to have a good broker be it a person you deal directly with or an online broker; researchers help to narrow down the amount of time you spend on finding shares and doing your own investigations before you invest.

When building your teams you need people you can trust. People whose advice you respect. Ultimately, though, it is you who is going to make the final decision on your investment. So put your team together, listen to what they have to say but remember it is your money that is being invested and ultimately it is your money that will be lost if you make an incorrect decision. Listen to what others say but make up your own mind.

When I was building my property portfolio up to 2007, I had a great team of people working around me. They had by this stage worked with me for a few years and understood exactly what I wanted. The estate agent knew the type of properties I wanted and would normally ring me just before a house went on public sale. Once I had viewed it and made an offer they sent the contract direct to my broker and solicitor. The broker and solicitor had all my details and the loan was in place within hours. The contracts were completed within days.

Once the purchase had completed the tradesmen had moved into the property to refurbish it. They could turn a property around in 4 weeks and that included new kitchen, new bathroom, new carpet and full decorated.

In the final week the broker would have a new mortgage at the higher value in place with the solicitor just waiting for the go ahead. A tenant would be waiting to move in. By the end of week 4 the new mortgage was completed, tradesmen moved out onto the new property and a tenant moved in.

For the whole process I would spend about 30 minutes working on the deal. Because I had such a great team around me I only needed to see them when they needed a signature. They were all professionals in their respective fields.

Building a great team takes time but the results are magical when you have everyone working together for your best interest.

Mentors

Mentors are those great people who provide the road map to your success. They inspire, motivate, and provide information, fun and entertainment. Their books, dvd's, workshops and seminars are always around and easily referred to when you get distracted, feel things are not quite going your way or when you are having a great time and need guidance on getting to the next level in their speciality.

During my work day I use lots of tools and information provided by my mentors. My daily/monthly/annual planner is adapted from a system created by Paul J Meyer for personal productivity. Each day I set aside some time to read a chapter from whatever book I am reading at the time. (Reviews can be found on http://newydd105.blogspot.co.uk including reviews of my own books as they are due for publication.)

Dvd's are always playing in the background some of my favourites are Anthony Robbins, Robert Kiyosaki, Napoleon Hill, Zig Ziglar, Paul J Meyer and Darren Hardy. Sometimes they are turned down quite low and just audible other times such as when I am on the treadmill or in the gym they are turned up quite loud. Subconsciously, I gain something each time they are played even though I am not always concentrating on them.

I'm a strong believer that if you find someone who is successful at what you want to do then copy what they are doing. They have obviously found a system that works. It works for them and there is no reason to suspect it won't work for you. Don't be afraid to copy what they do after all, they have already made all the mistakes that will hopefully reduce your errors and help you achieve your success quicker.

Some of my mentors don't even know they have helped me achieve my success. Here are some of them:

Robert Kiyosaki – author of the Rich Dad, Poor Dad series of books. I've read every book he has written and learnt something new from each one. I've reread the books over and over again and each time I get more information from the books. I've attended 3 seminars and a weekend workshop run by Robert or his team. Each time I get something new to work with. I met Robert once before I started on this financial journey. Does he know how much he has helped me I would have to say no. He probably doesn't even remember I exist but he is the mentor who has had the most impact on my financial education and building my lifestyle.

Brad Sugars – Author of the book Instant Cashflow and owner of Action Coach. The book totally altered my outlook on running and buying a business. The business chassis formula in its day was revolutionary. I've attended one of Brad Sugars seminars and employed an Action Coach to help me with one of my earlier business. Does Brad Sugars know how much he has helped me? The answer would again be no. But he is an important mentor to me for business structure.

Kevin Green – Kevin is most famous for his television appearances on Secret Millionaire and Dinner with the Devil. Kevin runs seminars and workshops around the world. I attended one of Kevin's weekend workshops and got lots of ideas from him. Quite by chance I've met Kevin a couple of times and always have a chat with him. Does he know how much he has helped me? He knows he has pointed me in a direction a few times but probably doesn't realise how much those little hints have helped. But Kevin always remembers me and makes a point of saying hello.

Andrew Reynolds - Andrew is one of the geniuses of Niche Marketing. I've attended some of his weekend workshops and subscribed to his monthly Cash-On-Demand training program. I've also emailed Andrew on several occasions when I've needed some guidance when something didn't quite work out as I planned and he would point me in the right direction. As with Kevin Green, Andrew will know he has helped me but not to the extent of the success I have achieved from those hints and ideas.

Jimmy Chapman – Jimmy is a very successful Network Marketer. I joined a network marketing business with no sponsor. I just saw a business opportunity that I thought would compliment my existing business and investments. Jimmy contacted me, took me under his wing and now helps me with building my network marketing business. He is just a telephone call away. He sends me weekly emails and updates and has given me some good ideas on incorporating things I want to achieve into this business model. Does he know how much he has helped me? He probably doesn't know. He will see how I'm building my network marketing business but he doesn't know he has given me some ideas that help other areas of my businesses and investments.

Warren Buffett – Warren is regarded as one of the greatest, if not the greatest, share investor. Having the title of the Richest Man in the World for many years he has given billions away to charities and is now around the 3rd richest man. He produces annual letters to his shareholders which have become legendary in their advice to investing in the share market. Each year you can bid for a lunch with Warren and in 2011 it would only cost you 2 million dollars to win the bid. Warren's ex-daughter-in-law has written several books on Warren's investment style and strategy. Excellent books which have helped me with my share investments. Does he know how much he has helped me? The answer has to be a resounding no. He would have no idea who I am. But he has been one of my mentors for many years.

Paul J Meyer – Through an organisation know as LMI – leadership Management Institute – I was first introduced to Effective Personal Productivity. This is a system of managing your productivity, time and achieving goals and success. Through this program I used the Planner for daily, monthly and annual goals, changing bad habits and tracking progress. Did Paul J Meyer knew how he had influenced my day to day habits the answer is no. Even though he is no longer with us his teachings continue to have an impact on my daily routine.

I hope you can see from the list above that mentors don't need to know you personally to be a mentor to you. It's nice to have some mentors you can call, email or text when you get stuck or unsure of yourself. But books like this one or any of the recommended reading books can be a type of mentoring for you.

Following the right people on social networks like Facebook and twitter can be your mentors as well.

You can follow me on:

Twitter @newydd105

http://newydd105.blogspot.co.uk

www.karennewton.co.uk

The Karen Newton Mentoring Program

In 1999 I read Rich Dad, Poor Dad by Robert Kiyosaki and got very excited about the possibilities and opportunities explained in the book. In early 2000, we were living in New Zealand and my husband and I travelled for five and a half hours from our home town to Auckland to hear Robert Kiyosaki speak and then travelled home again. Eleven hours spent travelling to listen to a speech that lasted about 2 hours.

On the way home my husband and I talked non-stop about the possibilities that were presented to us. We were so excited we took another day off from our business to read Robert's new book 'Rich Dad's Guide to Investing'. By the end of the day we had a plan.

We tried to implement the plan but it didn't go as we had hoped. New Zealand has a very high home ownership and when we talked to lenders about borrowing for rental properties we received resounding no after no. We then decided our plan would work better in Australia. They have a much larger population and higher rental market. We packed up and moved to Australia. Again things did not go according to our plan. We had been in Australia for only a couple of days when my mother who lived in the UK died. We travelled to Britain. The next eight months were taken up with hospital visits and funerals as I lost six family members.

During this time I got a job and so did my husband. We still talked about our plans and are evenings were filled with walks around the town centre looking at property for sale in every real estate agents office. On weekends we would visit the offices, talk about wanting to build a property portfolio and pick the brains of any agent willing to give us a few minutes of their time.

We talked to bank managers who sadly all said 'forget it'.

But we persevered and one year later bought our first property. It wasn't a rental but a home for us to live in. Three months later we bought our first rental property. Then we got side tracked. We were both working and had little or no time to work on our plan. We finally, came to realise our plan was the most important thing to us. Nothing was going to stop us achieving it. So my husband gave up his job to concentrate on building a rental portfolio full time. I worked on the other aspects of the plan in my free time. Within 3 years I was able to leave the job I had and work full-time on our plan.

Lucky for us both my husband and I were able to motivate and support each other and have the mutual determination to make our plan work. Many people don't have someone encouraging them along the way and eventually they give up.

For this reason, I run a 12 month mentoring program. I guarantee at the end of the 12 months you will be wealthier and have better income than when you started on my program provided you are willing to put in the effort needed.

From day one I will help you identify where you are currently with your finances, the areas that need to be worked on and introduce you to your first strategic step towards financial independence. At the end of the 12 months you will have gained substantial knowledge and be wealthier and have better cashflow. You will have direct contact with me via email and telephone as well as a monthly one on one meeting.

I will help you put together a plan that identifies what you want to achieve. Then I will act as your mentor and coach. I'll be there to keep you on track with your plan for 12 months by which time you will have learned and earned enough that your successes should be enough motivation to keep you going.

You can get further information by emailing me info@karennewton.co.uk please put mentor in the subject line.

After 12 months the support doesn't stop. We just move into a different stratosphere where you can join our elite club and get exposure to larger and more sophisticated investment opportunities.

Everyone needs a mentor whether a personal mentor to keep them on track or mentoring through books, dvd's, workshops and seminars. The more support you have the greater your successes will come.

Section 1 - Summary

Congratulations on getting this far with the book.

In this first section we've looked at understanding financial jargon from an investor's viewpoint. You should now understand the difference between good debt and bad debt and that you can use good debt and leverage to buy income producing assets.

We've discussed the difference between liabilities and assets and how building a portfolio of income producing assets can make you wealthier and improve your cashflow.

We've looked at some of the skills you need to start your financial journey and we've also covered some of the tools that can help you along the way such as using compounding interest; leveraging; cycles and the use of mentors to keep you on track.

I hope you are now ready to get on to section 2 and get into the nitty gritty of making money.

Section 2

How to Make Money

Section 2 - Introduction

In the next section of this book we will look at how to start making extra money and building the investments that will help you survive 2012 and beyond.

In writing this section of the book, I have used actual examples of my investments. I have done this, not to show off how wealthy I am but so you can see how the investments work and how they can impact on your net worth and income. After all, the aim of this book is to increase both these areas of your finances.

One of the patterns you will see throughout the investing section is that I believe in setting aside regular monthly amounts for each investment. When I first started working on my financial plan £10 was a lot to set aside each month but as I slowly built up my income this was increased to £100 then £200, £500 and so on. What I am trying to show you is that you can start with a small amount of money even if you can only spare £10 per month to start with and you can gradually build it up to more as you reduce your debt and increase your income. If £10 is too much for you then start with £5 per month or even £1. Anyone can start with any amount they want. The main thing is to start doing something now.

Learning about investing and physically investing is a life long journey. The world we live in is continually changing and the investment world keeps changing with it. We must continue to learn and adapt to the changes as best we can.

You have started by reading this book. I hope you take the action necessary to put into practice what you are learning. You don't get anything for nothing. If you don't put in the effort then you won't get the results.

Simple little steps taken each and every day will add up to fantastic results.

When I'm writing it is easy to say I'll do that tomorrow and never get around to doing it. Sometimes I would start a book and simply not finish it. I'd get distracted and not get around to doing anymore writing. Other times I would start a book get an idea for another book and lose interest in the first book. To overcome this I started planning time each day to write. An hour a day had a book finished very quickly, edited and ready for print. These days one hours writing a day is still a very good habit. If I am not working on a book then it is writing a review for my blog site, updating information on my website or just updating my journal. Writing for an hour each day is now part of my daily routine and over a year produces an enormous amount of written work.

Saving and investing is similar. You have to set aside the time to read information, digest it and make a decision on what you want to invest in. Getting into the habit of setting aside a certain amount of time each day over a year will add up to a lot of information collected and digested. You might not have an hour a day it might be 20 minutes is all you can spare. 20 minutes a day over a week is 140 minutes or 2 hours of reading.

Little steps taken each and every day can give massive results.

Net Worth

Throughout the book you will be reading about Net Worth. This is what I use to define how wealthy a person is. Someone can easily say today I'm a millionaire simply because they own their own home in a certain part of the country. They are correct on paper they are a millionaire but if you look at their finances their house may be worth £1million but they may have a £500,000 mortgage, they may have a £20,000 car loan, £5,000 credit card, store cards of £1000 etc. And when you add up all the debts it comes to £526,000. Minus that from the £1million value of their home and their net worth becomes £474,000. This to me is not a millionaire. If they were forced to sell everything then they would end up with considerably less than a million pounds. This is the reason I talk about net worth. The aim of this book is to increase your net worth which is where the true wealth lies.

Cashflow

Cashflow or Income is again a net figure. If in your job your take home pay is £1000 a month and you spend £1000 a month then your cashflow is zero. If you take home £1000 and you spend £800 then you have positive cashflow of £200. The aim of this book is to help you increase the amount of positive cashflow you have each month. As you build the cashflow then you have more money available to invest and this in turn provides you with more cashflow. Eventually, you can build enough cashflow from your investments that you no longer need your job and you can become financially free.

So let's get started on the journey.

A Plan

So far throughout this book you will have read about the plan and wondered what I was talking about. The plan is a statement my husband and I put together detailing what we wanted to do and how we were going to achieving it.

Businesses have a Business Plan. It provides information on the history of the business, what it has achieved in the past, what it hopes to achieve in the future and how it intends to get there. The plan is unique to each business.

I believe that anything that is important in your life should have a plan. Therefore, I have a financial plan. As you know, I like to keep things simple and unlike a business my plan doesn't run into pages and pages of information. It consists of only a couple of lines.

For me the plan is my guide for the future and it is also the reference point that I keep coming back to. I don't have time to read 20 or 30 pages of information in a traditional business plan. I want something that will just remind me of what I have set myself to achieve in a short a number of words as possible.

We wrote our financial plan in 1999 and still have the same plan today. Only one thing has changed. I had a date by which time I was going to achieve the plan. The date has been removed. I set a date of 2009 to achieve the plan. I thought 10 years was a reasonable period to work at building my wealth and income. I achieved the plan in 2003. Now the plan is there as a reminded of what I wanted to achieve, how I wanted to achieve it and gives me the tools to keep expanding my future net worth and income.

My plan reads:

To achieve financial freedom and generate passive income through investments including shares, rental property, book royalties and business income.

That is my financial plan. It is a very simple plan. It is a plan that works. It reminds me everyday what I need to do to build my net worth and increase my income. If I digress I take a look at the plan and come back to the basics – buy some shares, rent out a property, write a book and build a business. These are four very simple steps to building wealth.

As we move through the money making section of the book I hope you will find sufficient information to help you put together your own plan. If you can't come up with one then feel free to use mine.

Ideally, you should have a date to aim for. It could be 1 year in the future or 5 years or a 10 year plan. Write down all the ideas you have and don't worry about how stupid or unrealistic they may see at the moment. The main thing is to get them down on paper. Now look at setting goals and with each goal some steps on how to achieve your goal. If you want it bad enough you will soon find a way to achieve it.

When I started my property portfolio I set a target of doubling the number of properties I bought each year. In year one I planned on buying one property. In year 2 I would buy two properties. In year three I would buy four properties and so on. I remember looking at the plan and wondering how on earth I was going to get enough money together for my first property let alone buy four properties in a year. But a remarkable thing happened, once I focused on getting the first property I worked out a system that allowed me to buy a second property and then a third one. Between 2001 and 2007 I bought 60 properties.   Not quite the double each year but I'm not complaining about having 60 properties.

If I hadn't put the plan together and worked hard on it how many properties do you think I would own today? The answer is probably zero.

I could still be saying to myself I can't find a deposit. I can't find a mortgage. What if I can't find a tenant for the property? There are a million excuses I could make not to get into rental property. However, by having a plan and taking one step at a time how many properties could you own in 10 years time?

With shares I had a plan to increase my income through dividends by a set amount each year. I started with £50 pounds a year and increased it to £100 then doubled it again to £200 and so forth. Small steps increased each year to produce an income that stands at £10,000 a year in dividends. My aim is to now double that to £20,000 a year and so on. How easy would it have been to say 'I'm not going to invest in shares it is too risky' or the common misconception 'I need £10,000 to start a portfolio.' Small simple steps over time and you too could be earning a similar amount. Open an ISA and if you don't have much money start with £10 per week or £10 per month. When you have £100 buy some income producing shares. Invest the dividend back into you ISA and keep going until you have the next £100 and so on. Don't make excuses as to why you can't invest. Instead, become a 'can do' expert and find a way to make it happen.

Likewise in my lending portfolio, I started lending £10 per week, then £20 per week then £40 per week. As the interest return and income increased so did the amount invested back into the lending portfolio until I reached the maximum I could legally invest under current laws. When the amount increase this year so did the amount I put into the lending portfolio.

Again simple little steps have compounded over time to produce enormous results.

Start your own plan today and put together 3 simple steps you can take each day, each week or each month. If you are setting aside money do it by standing order either weekly or monthly. It doesn't need thinking about and adds up very quickly to a large sum of money invested over a year.

Whatever, you decide to do find the reason you are going to do it instead of making excuses why you can't do it.

When I was a kid and I would say 'I can't do it' my dad would give me a dictionary and tell me to look can't up in it. In those days there was no such word as can't in a dictionary. When I told him I couldn't find the word he would say 'that's because there is no such word as can't. There are only two reasons you can't do something either you don't want to do it or you don't know how to do it. If you don't know how to do it then I will teach you and if I don't know how to do it we'll learn together. If the real reason is you don't want to do it, tough, go and do it now.'

Without realising it I was learning a fantastic lesson. Don't put anything off until tomorrow get it done today and if I don't know how to do something then go and learn how to do it. No excuses just have a 'can do' attitude.

Reducing Debt

Before we get into making money it is important to ensure personal debt is under control. If you have credit cards, store charge accounts, loans, hire purchase etc. you need to put a plan together to reduce the debt as quickly as possible. Allow about 5 years to get rid of all the debt. I would allow a longer period of time if you have a high debt level. Be realistic about setting your targets to reduce the debt.

There is no easy way of reducing debt. It is just a case of having good discipline and just doing it. I have found the best way to start is with credit cards. That's because the ratio between interest and capital alters each month and you can see a reduction taking place each month in the amount you still owe. This is a good motivator to keep you going. Work out how much extra you think you can add to the monthly repayments. An extra £10 doesn't seem much today but in a few months time you'll be surprised at the results.

If you have several cards the trick is to pay extra off just the one card while maintaining minimum payments on the other cards. Once card one is paid off the repayments you were making should be applied to the second card and so on until all cards are cleared. The first card is the most difficult to clear after that you have a large sum that can be paid off card two and that one reduces quicker. As an example credit card one has a repayment of £150 per month and credit card two also has a repayment amount of £150. You have £20 extra available to pay off card one so the total amount now being paid off credit card one is £170 per month. Once that card is cleared you add the £170 to the payments you are making on credit card two. Your total payment on credit card two now becomes £320. Applying the full £320 to card two will reduce it much quicker than card one. Again you are applying the compounding effect only this time you are using it to reduce debt. Whatever you apply the compound effect to you will have incredible results.

Once you have cleared the cards put them away in a safe place. Don't carry them with you as that just puts temptation in your path and you may use them again. You don't want bad debt going back on the cards again. The next time you use your cards you will want to use them for good debt and we'll cover that later in the book.

It is very important to be able to manage your money carefully. Once you have created more income then you can spend a little more on personal extravagances. My advice is get into the habit of paying cash for everything. When you pay by cash and the wallet or the purse looks empty then you don't spend so much. Dealing in cash is a good way of helping you to manage your money more carefully.

A little trick I learned a long time ago was to have 3 jars. Label the first one debt, the second investing and the third charity. At the end of each day empty your pockets or purse of all the change you have and split it evenly between the three jars. At the end of the month take the money from the debt jar and use it to make an additional payment on your credit card. Take the money from jar 2 and pay it into an investment account. Give the money in jar 3 to a charity of your choice.

Keep this process going until all the debt is cleared. Once that is done the debt jar becomes an investment jar. So you have two-thirds of the money going to investments and one third going to charity. You'll be surprised how much additional money you find each month.

Another trick I learned was to keep a small notebook in my handbag and every time I bought something I would write it down in the notebook. It is amazing how annoying that habit becomes and you will do almost anything not to have to get the notebook out and write down the purchase. It is a good way of controlling your expenditure.

Charity

I'm a great believer in giving to charity. You will find that most wealthy people also give large sums of money to charity.

It always amazes me that those who give so freely always seem to receive freely. I'm not saying give to charity just to receive. But there seems to be this balance in life that when you give you receive.

There are many charities that would welcome any donations they can get and often not just money. My old quilts and cushions go to a dog rescue centre. There are many charities that take clothes, shoes, books, furniture, washing machines, fridges, toys the list is endless.

I have a habit that each day I walk around the house and I throw something out. We all tend to hoard things and I'm as bad as the next person. But I now make a conscious effort to throw something out. This week an old pair of favourite shoes went into the recycling bag. Several items of clothing also joined the shoes. Magazines that I have kept just in case I need some information found there way to some doctors and dentist surgeries. The old computer screen went to a local shop for parts. Everything has been given away free of charge for someone else to get a benefit from. Why don't you try it? One item a day.

If you are undecided about which charities to donate your 3rd jar of money to, my three favourite charities are RNLI; Air Ambulance and Help for Heroes. Why not make a list of 12 charities and donate to a different one each month.

Get A Business

The next important step for Surviving 2012 is to get a business. This really should be non-negotiable. A business is a legitimate way of reducing your tax bill. A company can be used for legal protection as well as financial protection.

The so called super-rich, use businesses as a way of protecting their wealth and reducing tax liability. Many well paid employees of government departments use a company system to reduce the tax they pay on their high income.

Let's take a look at the tax benefits of having a business. If you have a job then your money is taxed at source via PAYE (Pay As You Earn). That is you pay tax before you receive your wage. Have a look at your payslip and see how much is taken in PAYE tax and NIC contributions. Other deductions may apply such as a pension contribution. The main thing is the government gets paid first in the form of taxes and you receive what is left.

If however, you have a business you can offset business expenses before any tax is taken and this in turn reduces the amount of tax payable and gives you more money in your hand – or in other words an increase in your income.

If you have a business that you run from home you can claim part of your house as a business expense so you can charge part of your gas, electricity, council tax, telephone to your business expenses. Depending on the business you have you may be able to claim for some of your car expenses.

One of my businesses is rental properties. I run my business from home. I am therefore entitled to claim part of my mortgage as a business expense, part of my gas, electricity and water are also claimed. I have Council Tax to pay and part of that is also paid for by the business. As my rental business involves visiting tenants and doing inspections on the property; showing prospective new tenants properties available for letting and having to collect rents from some tenants then transport is a very important part of my business. I am therefore able to pay from the business some of the petrol; some of the road tax and a proportion of the insurance costs. All of these legitimate expenses help to reduce my tax burden.

I am not advocating tax avoidance because that is illegal. What I am trying to show you is that there are many legal expenses that can be paid for by the business. If you have a limited liability company then tax is paid at a lower rate than if you were taxed as an individual.

At the time of writing this book corporation tax is charged at 26% with the chancellor hoping to reduce corporation tax to 23% by 2014. On the other hand individual tax rates go up to 50% depending on how much you earn.

This is the reason so many actors, singers, writers, investors and government employees have limited liability companies.

JK Rowling who is the author of the Harry Potter books receives royalties for every book sold. She has also been paid for the rights to her books to turn them into very successful movies. She receives a percentage of the profit from the movies. In addition she received royalties for all the merchandising relating to Harry Potter. I'm also sure she has some sort of licence fee or royalty scheme in place to benefit from the theme parks opening soon. The Sunday Times Rich List gives JK Rowling a wealth of £126 million. She has a limited liability company and it pays tax at 26% on the profits made after all her legal expenses are deducted. Imagine how much poorer she would be if she had been taxed as an individual at the 50% tax rate.

Make having a business your number one priority before getting into any other investments detailed later in the book.

If you are unsure about starting a business or want to start a business but have little or no idea where or how to start then contact me on info@karennewton.co.uk I should be able to help you get started.

Where does your income come from?

Robert Kiyosaki is for me one of the greatest financial teachers of our generation. He is the author of the Rich Dad, Poor Dad series of books. I recommend reading as many of them as you can. Throughout his books he talks about what he refers to as the cashflow quadrant. The Cashflow Quadrant helps you to understand where your income comes from. By understanding where you are in the quadrant, where your income is generated you can plan how to move into different quadrants that have far more benefit to helping you create more income, greater wealth and keep it.

Robert Kiyosaki says there are for quadrants and they are named as E quadrant, S quadrant, B quadrant and the I quadrant. An explanation of the meaning of each quadrant and where your income comes from is described as:

E = Employee, some one who has a job, they receive wages and are taxed before they receive their money.

S = Self Employed or a small business owner employing a few staff. In this type of business you get some of the tax benefits but you still have to work everyday to receive any money. Generally, everybody gets paid before you do. If you take time off from your business it will grind to a halt.

B = Business Owner, this is the type of business that employs 500 or more staff. You have managers who work for you. You do not work in the business. An example would be Richard Branson who, the last I heard, had around 300 companies. It is impossible for him to work in each company so he has managers to run his companies. Another type of business which Robert Kiyosaki includes in this category is a network marketing business. A network marketing business has the potential to grow very quickly and provide residual income as you build your customers and distributors. (Network Marketing is included in another chapter)

I = Investor, your money comes from the income earned from your investments. Investments such as rental properties and shares are included in this category.

To create financial freedom for yourself, you need to receive the bulk of your income from the B and I quadrants. It is possible to become financially free if you are self-employed or working for someone. However, true wealth comes from being a business owner and an investor. It comes from having money come in whether or not you are working. With the rental properties I receive the rents on the 1st of each month. The money is usually paid direct to my rental bank account. In some cases I have to chase tenants for the payment but normally good tenants ensure their rent is paid into my account on the due date. I don't have to go to work to receive the money it is paid each and every month that I have a tenant in the property.

With the shares that I own, the dividend is paid into my bank account on dividend settlement day. I don't have to chase the company for the payment it automatically gets paid into the account.

Every month I receive commission payments from the network marketing business that I operate. Again, I don't have to chase the company for the money it automatically goes into my account.

I could be on a beach in the South of France and the money would still go into my account each month. That is financial freedom, being paid each month without even being in the country.

Being able to increase and continue building my wealth every month with little or no input from me.

This book will show you how to do that. In addition, I recommend reading Robert Kiyosaki's books Cashflow Quadrant and Unfair Advantage.

Starting a business?

The type of business you decide to set up is really up to you. You may have a hobby that can turn a little profit your way. You may want to run a small retail outlet or have dreams of building your own chain of shops.

It is never too late to start a business. Often I hear excuses such as I'm too old or I can never do that. Well, Colonel Sanders of KFC fame was in his 60's when he started building the Kentucky Fried Chicken franchise. If you are alive and breathing then it is not too late to start you business venture.

If you don't have the skills or knowledge to start a business then learn. There are always training courses run through local banks, councils or even private courses through my own mentoring program.

Start a small business and grow it a little bit each day.

Simon Dolan wrote in his book 'How to make millions without a degree', about starting a business and how to build it. Simon Dolan is the owner of SJD Accountancy a multi-million pound business. A business he built step-by-step from scratch. As he says in his book -

..There's a good reason millionaires don't detail their rise from thousands to millions. It's because the story is boring. Businesses grow little by little; year by year...most millionaires grow their fortune bit by bit."

Simon Dolan is now credited with being worth in the region of £100 million. In addition to his accountancy firm he has a car racing business, an aviation business, a publishing business and more. He has also managed to build a lifestyle many would be envious of.

But before you rush in to starting your business take another look at the quadrants as defined by Robert Kiyosaki and which quadrant/s you want to earn your income from. Where do you want to be earning most of your income from? Hopefully, you realise the greatest wealth comes from the B & I quadrants and that is where you will also want your wealth to come from.

For me I earn most of my income from the B and I quadrants with the exception of my books.

In the B quadrant I have several businesses such as the publishing business, solar panel business, network marketing etc. My investments are property, shares, bonds, and lending. However, I am self employed (S quadrant) when I write my books. Why am I self employed because if I don't write them they will grind to a halt and not be written at all. The production of my product, my book, is dependant 100% on me. No me, no book, no royalties being received.

As I said previously most of my income comes from the B and I quadrant with the largest portion of my income being in the I quadrant.

Business Types

There are three types of business.

1. The first business is one that starts off from scratch as a small business which you invest time and money into building. It starts small but grows and you invest the time into working your business.   I've done this. Run a business from a spare room/bedroom and built it up to employ 20+ staff, needing premises and having massive overheads. The hours were long

and the stress high. While I initially enjoyed it as it grew bigger it became more difficult to run and manage. The hours became longer and I hated having to deal with staff that were sick, having time off and not performing. From the small business owners I have spoken to this is a constant problem. There are people who thrive in this environment and have very successful small businesses. You may be one of them. If you have the knack for building and managing a business then this type of business may suit you. It is also the type of business that can be built up to become a B type business where you employ 500 or more staff. Richard Branson is a great example of a true B type business owner. The Virgin brand has around 300 companies. Richard Branson can't manage all of them so he employs people who are good at what they do and good at making him money.

2. The Franchise – this is where you buy a successful business model and set it up in your region. With a franchise you are buying a licence to use a well known name and have access to business support and training. There are numerous franchises selling practically everything you can imagine. Some of the franchise names that come to mind are McDonalds, Cartridge World, Century 21 Estate and Letting Agents, Shell Petrol Stations and Cash Converters. These are successful businesses. In a franchise you pay a sum of money to buy a license and have the right to use the franchise name and product.   You pay an advertising fee, a lease fee and there are other fees paid whether your business is successful or not. Franchising is a growing business model and very popular. It may or may not suit your needs.

What if you reversed this idea and built your own franchise? Let's say your business idea is to sell cupcakes you have made yourself. You start selling them in your shop and they are very successful. You put together your favourite recipes and your system for making and icing the cakes. You now have a business you can sell. There are people around the country who may want to own a cupcake business but don't know how to cook them or how to run a business. They decide to buy a licence from you to use your name, your recipes and your system. Now you have a franchise and your business is growing bit by bit.

So instead of buying someone else's franchise you are now the proud owner of your own franchise. Sounds easy doesn't it.

3. Network Marketing – if you read my blogs (www.karennewton.co.uk/blog or

newydd105.blogspot.com) you will see I write a lot about the growth of the cottage industry. These are small businesses run from home. Network Marketing falls into this category. It is a small extremely successful growing industry run from home but with the support of a major company. You can put in as much or as little time as you want to. The business is about building a network of customers and a network of distributors. Distributors being like minded business people who want to build their own business. The start up costs are low with enormous rewards available. Some of the wealthiest people have made their money from this type of business. Network Marketing is a smaller version of a Franchise without the on going costs associated with having a franchise. A good network marketing company provides excellent training and support. For anyone who has little or no business experience it is a great way to get started.

I have a network marketing business with Telecom plus. The business sells gas, electricity, telephone, broadband and mobile phones. With my rental properties this adds a nice extra income from the properties. The company provides good training, excellent products and fantastic opportunities.

As with any business or investment allow yourself a minimum of 5 years to establish yourself and get to know business or investment thoroughly. With a network marketing business you can start with a small sum of money to join the business and commit as little or as much time as you choose. For me the time is minimal being about 1 hour a month but my business is starting to grow nicely and produce a good little income growing steadily each month. The more time you put into the business the quicker it will grow. Remember Simon Dolans words and grow your business bit by bit, day by day. You don't need to rush out and trying and build your business within the first month then run out of steam because you aren't getting the results you need or expect. A slow steady pace over a long period of time will always produce better results.

Several years ago the government introduced FIT (Feed In Tariff) for houses with Solar Panels encouraging their installation as part of the renewable energy targets the world is working towards. Telecom plus pay a higher rate of FIT then the government pays. This is another reason I chose this network marketing business because with my rental properties every time I install solar panels on the roof of a rental property I get the FIT.

This little network business is an added bonus to what I already do increasing my income from my properties and because I manage my properties myself I sell the service to my tenants so there is very little additional work required to bring in a nice monthly income.

The beauty of a network marketing business is that there are no restrictions on how big a business you can grow. With 70 millions people in the UK and continually growing, I am sure you can find a few customers to make your business successful.

With such an enormous potential for growth it is easy to see why a network marketing business is classed as a B quadrant business.

If you want further information then email me at info@karennewton.co.uk and put telecom plus in the subject line.

Taking Action

Last year we were out for dinner with some friends who run their own manufacturing business. My daughter had taken part in a school activity called 'the tenner project'. Every child in her school year was given the opportunity to run a business. They had to provide a business plan to the teacher and they were given £10 each to buy the stock for their business and run it for a month. At the end of the month if the business had made a loss then they still paid the £10 back to the teacher. If the business had made a profit they paid £11 back to the teacher and kept the profit. My daughter's business made a healthy profit. She was so excited that when we had dinner with our friends she started talking to them about all the different opportunities she had seen to start a business. Over dinner, writing on a napkin, she made a list of 15 businesses she would like to own. Some of the businesses will probably fall by the wayside but at least ten of those ideas could go on to be very successful businesses. They have to potential to be very successful franchises. My daughter has whittled her list down to four businesses she wants to start.

If my 12 year old daughter can come up with fifteen ideas after a month of trying to run her own business while at school then how many ideas could you come up with? Write them all down and see how many of them you can turn into successful businesses.

Why don't you do your own 'tenner project' challenge and see if you can start a business with £10 and run it for a month?   At the end of the month if it is successful keep going and slowly build it bit by bit, day by day.

If, however, you have genuinely put in an effort for a month and you feel the business is a failure close it down. All you have lost is £10 and some time and effort. You will have gained a lot of experience. Try and see where you think you went wrong and learn from the mistakes. Go back to your list of businesses and make a start on business number two on your list.

Network Marketing is another business opportunity that can be started instead of building your own business from scratch or it can be started as an additional business running alongside any business you start up. The training provided with a network marketing business will help you not only with your network marketing business but also with your start up business.

I'm with Telecom Plus and their fee for joining their network marketing group was £100. They run an incentive to refund your fee if you reach certain targets within 90 days of completing your introductory training. For me, I didn't attempt to meet the targets as I am the slowly bit by bit person who likes to plod along taking my time building my business slowly but surely. But I still managed to earn more than the cost of joining the company within the first two months of starting the business.

If you would like more information about Telecom Plus and would like to join my team you visit my website www.karennewton.co.uk or email me at info@karennewton.co.uk

Financial Pyramid

I use a Financial Pyramid as a way of ensuring a balanced array of investments. In the first section of this book I spoke about investment cycles. Cycles cover every type of investment and indicate when an investment product is in a growth or decline period.

The interesting thing about cycles is that investments don't all go up together or down together. They move at different times and for different lengths of time. For example in the UK property had a boom from 2000 up to 2007 and has been in decline since. For the Gold Cycle, Gold has been steadily going up for over a decade.

The benefit of understanding cycles is to buy when the investment is at its lowest. This is when the investment is usually at its cheapest point. It's like going shopping during the sales.

You are looking for the best deal at the cheapest price. The investments I look at are usually out of favour with journalist and financial advisors as my feeling is once you start reading about the investment in the newspaper then the best money has already been made in the investment. On the other hand I try to get out of a market when it is at its peak. I'm not always as successful as I could be. In 2001 I started buying shares as the share market was low at around 3200 for the FTSE100. In 2005, I thought the market had reached the top of the cycle and I sold all my shares for a healthy profit. I was wrong in my judgement and the share market continued to climb for a long time. There was a lot more money that could have been made. The thing is not to get too greedy. I had made a healthy profit so there was really nothing to complain about.

When I start reading things like property is going up and now is the time to buy, I know that now is the time for me to stop buying property and start looking at a different investment in a different cycle period. Once the masses start getting into an investment the opportunity to make large gains has gone. I also know it won't be too long before the bubble bursts. When I hear comments like the housing market is about to collapse I take it with a pinch of salt. Do my own research and buy when the figures make the most sense for my investment.

During the time I was buying property I frequently heard comments such as get out now the housing market is about to collapse. 'It is a sellers market rather than a buyers market. You are best to wait until the market changes.' I had had listened to every bit of advice offered during this time I would never have bought any property. In the song 'The Gambler' by Kenny Rogers the words are 'You gotta to know when to hold them, know when to fold them. Know when to walk away and know when to run.' The point there is YOU have to know not you have to listen to someone else telling you when to walk away or run. So don't listen to TV channels or newspapers when they advise the next best investment is xyz or your investment is about to collapse. Do your own research and have confidence in your decisions.

I like to vary my investments so when one is down in value another is up in value. This means I don't have exposure to just one area. For this reason I collect data on the investments I hold. I create my own cycle information from the data I collect. I have a very simple spread sheet in Microsoft Excel and create graphs from the data.

I keep a gold cycle spread sheet and earlier this year gold peaked around $1800 then moved back. I heard stories from everywhere saying gold had peaked and was on the way back done. My cycle charts told me differently and I continued to buy gold. My profits increased over the new couple of months. As I write this book in October 2011 the price of gold is still higher than the price at the start of the year. It may have peaked on one day at $1800 but the cycle chart still shows over the 10 months from January 2011 to October 2011 the price of gold at the end of each month has continued to show an increase on previous months.

Different financial institutions keep their own records and I have found that keeping my own gives me more confidence in my decisions based on my information. It is the same with the Financial Pyramid. Other financial institutions have their own version of a financial pyramid and I have my own. The one below is my version. You may like to look at other financial pyramids and as you build your knowledge try putting together your own version of the pyramid. But for the rest of this section we are going to work on my financial pyramid.

Building Your Pyramid

With the exception of the top of the pyramid –
the section called Speculation – I try add to each
of the other four sections every month. This
way I haven't concentrated on building just one
part of the pyramid. I have used a balanced
approach and spread my investments over
various sections.

Speculation

Growth

Income

Security

Foundation

What Makes Up My Financial Pyramid

Please don't confuse the word pyramid with a multitude of fraudulent schemes that are out there in the world of money. I have used a pyramid or triangle shape as being the norm in financial sector and because it is a very solid shape and our aim is to build a solid financial structure for our futures.

Foundation

In the foundation of my pyramid I have commodities. The commodities I currently hold are Gold, Silver and Copper. You can add other commodities (such as platinum, palladium, nickel, oil, gas etc.) or reduce them depending on their position in their investment cycle. For me I try to hold in the region of 5% - 10% of my wealth in commodities. As a commodity goes up in price I use the strategy of doubling my money whereby once a commodity has doubled in value I sell off half to recoup the investment I made. Holding onto the other half if I think it will still go up in value and buy another commodity currently out of favour and at the lower end of its investment cycle. I am still trying to keep the balance of 5%-10% of my wealth in commodities.

Security

The security section is as it says my security.   In this section I hold cash deposits this is money in the bank. Money invested in ISA and SIPP and government bonds. These are all fairly stable types of investments that have government guarantee if anything goes wrong with the organisation my money is held with. Banks now have £85,000 government guarantee per banking institution. You can hold up to one million in government bonds and are guaranteed the return of your money should there be any problems.

Income

This is the section that creates my income for the year. In this section I have businesses that I own outright and provide me with an income through wages or dividends. I have business in which I am a silent partner and receive a dividend from the investment. I have residual income which is generated through my network marketing business. I have royalties which are paid from my books. I receive rental income from the properties that I own. I have what is known as Blue Chip shares that pay a regular dividend and I run a lending portfolio and receive monthly interest from this.

Growth

In the growth section my investments are aimed at producing capital growth in the future rather than a regular income. So in this section I have investments in companies that qualify through the governments Enterprise Investment Scheme

(EIS). I invest in small companies listed on the stock exchange that are reinvesting all their money back into the business for future growth. I invest in exploration companies for gas, oil, gold etc.

Angel Investing is another growth potential where I supply money and/or expertise to a business in exchange for a negotiated return sometime in the future.

Property forms part of the growth section as I hope property will over a long period of time rise in value. When buying property my intention is not to sell. I am investing in property for the long term. The property that the Duke of Westminster holds has been in his family for generations. He may have sold some property and bought others but the Duke of Westminster holds an awful lot of property in the Westminster borough. It is my plan to be able to pass my properties on to my daughter and while I never say never, my intention is to hold the property indefinitely and be able to pass it on to future generations.

Speculation

This section is dedicated mainly to Spreadbetting. This is something I use very rarely. Because I trade very rarely I have yet to find a system producing a winning streak. Although I don't trade them I would include Forex, futures and options in this section.

So now you have my interpretation of a Financial Pyramid and I hope this gives you an overview of how I build up my overall portfolio of investments. Now let's look at some of these investments in more detail.

Foundation

Building Your Foundation

Commodities

Commodities form the foundation of the financial pyramid and the stability as I grow the assets. Commodities are such a simple investment anyone can invest in them.

A Good Starting Point.

Michael Maloney wrote a book 'Guide to Investing in Gold & Silver. Protect Your Financial Future'. If you are interested in commodities then it is as good a place as any to start learning about them. It also saves me pages and pages of writing explanations about commodities.

In his book Michael Maloney gives you a history of gold and silver. The book explains:

- Why commodities are one of the most profitable, easiest and safest investments you can make

- How the current economic crisis and the strategies of Central Banks such as Bank of England make your investment more profitable.
- Different ways you can invest in commodities

The book also gives a prediction for the future value of Gold and Silver. The book was published in 2008 and I find it very interesting how advanced Michael Maloney's theories were on World events. As I watch the world economies struggling in the current economic times I am fascinated with how the leaders of the various countries are reacting to the global economic situation as well as their own economies. Gold and silver go up and down depending on the decisions made by the leaders and rules have been implemented as Michael Maloney predicted they would. Maybe, it should be compulsory for any world leader to read his book. They may then think twice about the repercussions from their decisions.

Are Commodities A Safe Asset?

In truth commodities move a lot depending on the economics of the world. Since the 2008 Credit Crunch gold has been seen as a safe haven. A safe haven is seen as a way to protect your money and to provide some form of security against the falling value of sterling.

It was interesting to note the largest buyers of gold in the first 6 months of 2011 were the world's central banks. (That piece of information should be enough to make you want to find out more about commodities. What do the Central Banks know that no one else does?) The government in Venezuela banned the export of gold and demanded the return of all the gold it held overseas. Numerous countries put bans in place preventing large purchases of gold without having government approval to do so. In several states of America laws were passed making gold legal tender for paying for goods and services. In the Channel Islands you can open bank accounts that trade purely in gold and use those accounts for paying for your everyday purchases.

These are just some examples of how frightened Governments are that paper currency (also known as Fiat Currency) such as pounds, dollars and euros, is going to fail and become worthless. The governments of the world are preparing themselves for the worst possible scenario where fiat currency is worthless and those holding commodities become the wealthiest.

You have the opportunity to prepare yourself for the worst by investing in some commodities now.

How to Invest

The easiest way to invest in commodities is to buy from a bullion dealer. They can be found online. I recommend shopping around. I have two suppliers for Gold ingots, three suppliers for silver and another couple of suppliers for copper.

Last year when Central Banks were buying up large quantities of commodities I found my normal suppliers were unable to compete with the demand and were regularly out of stock. For that reason I've built up a network of suppliers who could fulfil my orders when needed.

Gold – I buy ingots from 1gram to 1 ounce depending on how much I want to increase my holdings by at the time. Bearing in mind I hold around 5%-10% of my total wealth in commodities. I buy or sell each month.

You may be surprised to find out how valuable your jewellery is. With the increase in gold values you could be sat on a fortune. A friend of mine inherited a pendant when her mother died. With all the talk about price increases she took the pendant to be valued and was amazed when the jewellery shop offered to buy the pendant from her for £2000. That was in 2007, I wonder what it would be worth today now that the price of gold has double.

Silver – I buy bullion coins usually the American Silver Eagle which is one of the most recognised coins in the world. The American Silver Eagle comes in two sizes either full size of one troy ounce or what is called half an eagle that is half a troy ounce. For around £20 you can buy half an eagle and it is a very easy way to get into investing. I also buy 100g ingot bars of silver. They are easier to store than having lots of coins around the place. Use your own judgement depending on how much silver you intend to hold and how much money you have available to start your investment.

It is estimated that there is less than 10 years worth of silver available in the world unless new mines are found. Silver is only mined as a by product of gold and no new mines have been found for many years. For this reason I believe silver is undervalued and could skyrocket in value in the future.

Copper – I hold both ingots and coins in copper. At todays prices you can get a lot for your money. Copper is seen as a gauge on how well the world economies are doing. As an industrial metal there is high demand when economies are booming and the value goes up. At present with economies declining the price is going down. Using our cycle charts now is a good time to buy as we are at a low in price values on the charts. As the world economies start to grow again the price will rise. It might not be for several years so there is a long timeframe of opportunity to build up your holdings.

Quality – When deciding on what to buy check the quality. You are looking for commodities that are .999 pure.

Storage – If buying small quantities then my suggestion is to store the commodities at home in a secure location or a home safe. When buying larger quantities if may be easier to store the commodities with an organisation specialising in this type of storage.

Other Ways to Invest in Commodities

Another way to invest in commodities is through the use of ETF's and ETC's. ETF is electronically traded funds and ETC means electronically traded commodities. This allows you to buy on margin. A caution with trading this way is the value of the ETF or ETC can go up or down. You can lose your money and end up having to pay more to settle the trade. Prices can move quickly and if you aren't keeping a close eye on them you money could go in seconds.

For me I prefer to physically hold my commodities but if you get into gas or oil etc. storage can be very difficult and expensive so an ETF or ETC would be the best option in those types of investments.

ETF/ETC Recommended Reading

There are numerous books available on trading in commodities using ETF and ETC. As I don't use this type of investment I will admit to only having read a couple of books about them. The only books I can actually recommend from my very limited reading on the subject are:

The Commodities Investor – Phillip Scott

High Powered Investing for Dummies

Security

The next section of our financial pyramid is security. In this section I include Life Insurance, Government Bonds, ISA and SIPPS and we will now look at each of these areas.

Life Insurance

For most of us our experience with insurance is strictly relating to home, contents and car insurance. These insurances are in place so if you have a car accident you are covered for damage to your car or third party vehicles. If your home is damaged through flood or fire then your home is repaired or if you lose something important such as jewellery, mobile phone, laptop etc. your content insurance will cover the cost. But insurances can also be used as a form of investment.

Whole of Life Insurance

A whole of life insurance is as it says an insurance for the whole of your life which is payable upon your death. Although you do not benefit from the insurance your next of kin will. You make small monthly payments for the remainder of your life and when you die your family or the person you nominate will receive the amount you are insured for from the insurance company.

In my circumstances I have a few whole of life insurance policies which are designated for specific purposes. These policies are reviewed as my circumstances change. Examples of the policies I have are:

- A policy to ensure if my home becomes mortgage free.
- A policy to ensure my daughter's school fees and university fees are paid allowing her to continue in formal education as long as she needs to without any disruption.
- A policy to cover the inheritance tax bill that my daughter will have. Under UK law the assets of a deceased are seized and held by the government until such time as the inheritance tax is paid. If

your plan is to sell off assets to cover the inheritance tax bill then you will need to think again as the government will not release any assets until the tax bill is paid. If you think your estate is going to be liable to inheritance tax this insurance will be an important part of your tax planning.

Life Insurance Policies with a Maturity Date

Maturity Date Life Insurance Policies are insurance that is taken out for specific period of time. You may decide to take out a policy for £10,000 which matures when you are 65 years old. So at the age of 65 you will get a pay-out of £10,000 plus any bonuses paid on the policy. If you die before reaching 65 years of age then your next of kin will receive the money upon your death.

I have a friend you every year starts a new policy which runs for 20 years. He started when he was in his 30's and his first policy for £5000 will pay out when he is 55 years old. He then has policies maturing every year for many years to come. £5000 may not seem a lot of money but it adds a nice little bonus to your annual income.

When I started this type of investment life cover of £5000 cost just a few pounds a month. Now the minimum cover seems to be for £20,000 but depending on your age £20,000 cover starts from as little as £5 per month. They are easily bought online.

The rate of return is not very good but they are not in my financial pyramid for their investment value but rather for the security they provide.

Bonds

When you purchase a bond you are lending money to the owner of the bond in exchange they agree to pay you interest on the amount you have lent them and they also agree to pay back your loan on an agreed date. You receive a certificate confirming the details.

Bonds are issued by many organisations and governments. In the UK governments bonds can be bought through NS&I (nsandi.com). They can be purchased small sums of money. Some allow you to contribute on a monthly basis and others require a lump sum payment. In return for receiving a loan of your money the government pays you interest on a regular basis.

Some bonds are designed to grow the capital you have invested while others are designed to provide you with a regular monthly income.

You have the choice of bond to suit your own circumstances.

Government Bonds as described above are guaranteed. You can invest up to £1 million and you will receive the money back in full – guaranteed.

Corporate Bonds

Many large businesses now use bonds as a way of accessing money for future developments within their business structure. It might be that the business wants to open new stores around the country but have insufficient capital to fund the expansion. They will arrange for bonds to be issued offering a certain interest rate. The interest payments are normally paid on a six monthly basis. The bond will run for a certain period anything from two years up to thirty years. At the end of the agreed period the business will pay back the full amount they borrow. Example – you lend the company

£10,000 at 3% interest for 10 years. Every six months you will receive interest payments of £150 and at the end of 10 years you will get back the £10,000.

Corporate Bonds are not guaranteed. If the business should fail you would become an unsecured lender and would have to wait and see if you received anything back once the company had been wound down.

If you are looking at Corporate Bonds you need to study more about them and the company you intend to invest in.

Councils

It is not uncommon for councils to use bonds as a way of obtaining funds for capital expenditure such as school improvements etc. They are not guaranteed but one likes to think a council is more secure than a business but then in the current economic climate – maybe not. It might pay to stick with government bonds instead.

ISA

ISA – stands for Individual Savings Account and is a wonderful product the government allows you to save your money in tax free. Every person from 18 years plus can open an ISA account.

There are two types of ISA.

- Cash ISA – as the product says this type of ISA is a cash investment. The maximum amount you can save for the year ended April 2012 is £5340. For year ended April 2013 it is £5640. The interest earned on the account is tax free and does not need to be declared on a tax return.
- The second type of ISA is a Stocks & Shares ISA. This investment can be in approved shares; gilts; bonds; mutual funds; ETF/ETC. They are a very flexible way of investing in other types of markets. The maximum investment amount for the year ended April 2012 is

£10,680 less any amount invested in a cash ISA. For the year ended April 2013 the maximum investment amount is £11,280 less any amount invested in a Cash ISA. The interest earned on the account is tax free and does not need to be declared on a tax return.

You should try to invest the maximum amount in an ISA each year. There are not many opportunities to invest and build a nice nest egg with no capital gains tax to pay.

This type of savings should not be underestimated as there is the potential to build millions in your ISA.

Recommended Reading

I recommend reading the following books about investors who have built the investment in their ISA's to over a million pounds.

The book 'Liquid Millionaire' by Stephen Sutherland while mainly a sales pitch book for his mentoring program does give some valuable insight into his investment strategies. His investments are mainly through Managed Funds and using a system he has put together you can move money from the Stocks and Shares component into the cash component of the ISA in the down cycle of the managed funds and back into the managed funds in an up cycle. It is a system that has created enormous tax free wealth for Stephen Sutherland in the region of hundreds of millions of pounds.

The book 'Free Capital' by Guy Thomas is a compilation of interviews he has with several investors who have used Stocks and Shares ISA to build more than a million pound in their ISA. Each of the interviewees has a different strategy for building their wealth. All the strategies can easily be applied to your own investment.

Junior ISA

The government has announced that from November 2011, it will be introducing a Junior ISA to encourage savings for children. The information available at the time of writing this book is that £3600 can be put into an ISA per year for a child. The money can come from parents, grand-parents aunt and uncles.

So far, it looks like the banks are not supporting the ISA's but they are available from other institutions.

SIPP

SIPP is a Self Invested Pension Plan which allows you to invest in a variety of investments tax free, very much like an ISA. The types of investments include commercial property, shares, funds, gold, gilts, bonds and many others. Unlike an ISA you can only access your funds when you reach 55 years of age.

Pension plans have a bad reputation not helped by governments changing the rules over and over again. But if you read the section on compounding interest you will know that a small amount saved each month started early enough in your working life can provide substantial amounts of money when you get to retirement age. Being in control of your own investment through a Sipp can provide numerous benefits.

A SIPP can be opened for a child and what an excellent way of helping them enjoy a better retirement life in the future. How many millions could be in a SIPP by the time your child is due to retire? If you are unsure re-read the section on compound interest.

More Information on SIPP

There are several organisations providing information, access and management of SIPP. An IFA (Independent Financial Adviser) can steer you in the right direction for further information on the types of investments you can put into your SIPP and what best suits your needs.

Income

This part of the financial pyramid is where I create my income and probably the part you are most interested in. I will go into this section in greater detail.

Building Your Income

I arrived in the UK in June 2000. I had moved from New Zealand to Australia in search of better investment opportunities to fit into the plan my husband and I had put together. But I had no money and had to wait 12 months before I could qualify for a mortgage to buy my own house or to obtain any form of credit.

I started working for a recycling company earning the minimum wage at the time of £3.60 per hour. My annual income came to £6926.40. My husband was occasionally employed to provide a little extra cash but most of the time we lived on my wage while he was free to start purchasing and renovating properties.

Today my income is around £27,000 a month equivalent to £324,000 a year and it continues to grow every month. I earn in one month what most people would like to be able to earn in a year. I live in a property with 3 acres of land running parallel to the canal. It is the type of property most people would dream of owning. I can afford to send my daughter to private school. I have holidays every time she is on school holidays and that is around 133 days a year. We spend Christmas at our apartment in the French Alps. I have an idyllic lifestyle that many can only dream about.

I am not saying this to brag but to show you what is possible by having a plan and working at it every day. I want you to understand that I started with absolutely nothing but by determination and perseverance I have built an income that anyone can achieve with a little bit of knowledge and support.

Remember my plan:

To achieve financial freedom and generate passive income through investments including shares, rental property, book royalties and business income.

My Goals are in the form to two questions:

1. What have I done today to improve my cashflow?
2. What have I done today to improve my net worth?

It hasn't been easy but it has been doable. Anyone with the same determination and desire to succeed can achieve the same and more.

So, let's take a look at the different investments that come under the Income section of my Financial Pyramid.

Business

To me having a business is the first most important step on the road to success. For many people though the thought of starting their own business can seem overwhelming and many will say 'definitely not me'. For those who don't want to start their own business or have no idea what to get into then the next section on Network Marketing may be of more interest to you.

This part is for those of you who have an idea for a business opportunity and would like to get it up and running.

Building Your Team

Accountant - As we've covered earlier in this book having a team can work miracles in your journey to Financial Freedom. When starting a business the first person to become part of your team will be an Accountant.

Your accountant will advise you on what records you need to keep. Do you need a computerised accounting program or will simply bank accounts be satisfactory for starting your business.

What sort of structure will suit you best? Do you need a Limited Liability Company or will being a sole trader or will a partnership be best suited to you.

Do you need to register for VAT? Do you need to pay NIC contributions? When do you need to submit tax returns? An accountant will be able to advise you on all the information you need to get started.

When I started investing in property, I interviewed many accountants until I found one who seemed to understand my expectations. They don't like being interviewed but the accountant I have has been my accountant for 12 years.

Bank – You will need a bank account for your business and most banks offer free business accounts for the first 12 months. That's ample time to start building your business and making some money. Some of the banks also offer training programs. It does pay to shop around and see who is offering what.

Solicitors – they offer advice or can put together contracts for your business. Do you have a product idea that needs protecting through copyright or patent protection? Again, interview solicitors until you get one that will operate within your timeframes.

I have gone through many solicitors and am still trying to find the right one for my business. I did have a firm which I stuck with for about 5 years. They were excellent to start with. Then they decided to expand their business to several towns and as the business grew they moved staff to other towns. As the staff changed the service deteriorated until they let me down badly. I couldn't get them to understand they were costing my business around £40,000 in poor service and not providing the timeframes I had become accustomed to. Unfortunately they had to go and I am back to again searching for a firm that can provide the service I expect.

Suppliers – What products are you selling to your customer and where do you source the product or materials from? You need to ensure your suppliers are capable to meeting your timeframes. You will also need to open accounts with them or do they deal in cash only accounts.

This is just an example of some of the people you will need as part of your team to get your business working and running smoothly. Obviously depending on the nature of the business depends on the people you will need.

Only you know the type of business you want
and what will be required to make it function
smoothly.

Why you need a business

We have covered in previous sections of this
book the need for a business. The main
advantage is tax. Having the ability to increase
your cashflow and reduce your tax will help you
to have more money available for your
investments.

When you work for someone you get paid on a
regular basis for the work you do. When you
receive your pay it already has tax and NIC
contributions deducted. What you get in your
hand is what you have to live on until the next
pay. From your money you have to pay all your
living expenses along with trying to find extra
money for investing.

When you have a business tax is paid after all the expenses are deducted from your profit. Tax is then payable on the balance. This has the effect of reducing your tax liability.

As a basic example say you have a wage of £500 and pay tax at 20% you would have tax of £100 and a balance of £400 to pay for your mortgage, gas, electricity, phone etc. As this is an example only I haven't included personal tax allowances.

Assume in your business you have just sold a product and after paying your supplier for materials you have £500 profit as your income. From the £500 you can deduct the cost of gas, electric, phone etc. In this case we are assuming the expenses come to £200. You are now left with £300 which is taxed at 20%. Your tax bill is £60. The balance in your hand is £240.

As an employee you brought home each month £400 but after paying gas electric, phone etc. at £200 you would be left with £200 in your hand. As a business owner you have £240 left an increase of £40 per month simply by having a business.

Most business when they first begin can incur start up costs and the business runs at a loss. The losses can be offset against your wages and you would have a tax code that ensures you pay lower taxes or zero taxes. This increases your cashflow giving you more money to start your investments.

An accountant will be able to explain all of this to you and help you get the best cashflow possible.

I am not advocating starting a business to lose money. Any business should be there to build, grow and eventually allow you to leave your job and run your business and investments full-time.

A book I would recommend reading is 'How to make millions without a degree' by Simon Dolan. Simon started a small accountancy business and then built the business to the extent that at the time of writing his book he was estimated to be worth £74 million.

What type of business can you start?

Every person will have their own ideas about the type of business they can run or would like to run. To get your mind thinking here is a list of businesses I and my husband have owned. Some sold, some closed down and some still running today.

- Welding
- Fire Protection
- Air Conditioning
- Electrical Contracting
- Security
- Banking consultancy
- ISO9001 consultancy
- Cosmetics
- Property
- Publishing

- Niche Marketing
- Solar Panels
- Mentoring
- Network Marketing

Action

For an exercise make a list of all the things you could do better in your job.

Make a list of all your hobbies and interests.

Can you find anything from your list that has the possibility of becoming a business?

Starting Your Business

A trap that a lot of people fall into is thinking they can't afford to start a business. It will take £20,000 to start or £100,000 and they don't have even £100 to get started. My advice is to start working your business from home where you do not have any overheads except for your time. Make the internet work for you it is fairly cheap to set up an online business. Write articles to promote your product on line or through newspapers and magazines. Use the social network sites to let people know you are in business. Use sites such as twitter, Facebook and LinkedIn to advertise your product and you. Use as much free advertising as possible.

If you have a computer print some fliers and walk the street delivering the fliers.

In March this year, my daughter, who was in year 7, was part of a school project called 'The Tenner Project'. It was voluntary and the plan was to run a business for one month. She had to come up with her own business idea and present it to the teacher. If the teacher liked it the pupil was given £10 to start their business. They were not allowed to use any money to start the business other than the £10 provided. After one month if their business was in profit they had to pay £11 back to the teacher and they could keep the profit. If, however, they lost money, they still had to pay £10 back.

My daughter's idea was to sell 'silly bandz' by bulk purchasing them, splitting them into sealed bags of 11 bandz and selling them for 50p. One more in a bag than if the kids bought them from a retail outlet. After one month she had made a profit of £50 and was quite delighted with her effort. One child in her school had an idea and made a profit of £900 from his £10 investment.

So the challenge is 'What could you start with £10?'

If you still have no idea for a business or don't like the idea of starting from scratch then a network marketing business may be ideal for you.

Network Marketing

We've mentioned earlier in the book about a network marketing business. Here I'd like to go into more detail about this type of business and how it can benefit you.

In the traditional type of business the employee gets a set wage for work done. The owners or shareholders of the business receive the profit and make most of the money.

In a network marketing business the structure is such that each person is self-employed running their own business. Each business has customers and distributors. Distributors are other people like you who want to run their own business. As a business owner you get paid based on the number of customers you have and how successful your distributors are. The person who introduces you to the business has a very simple job. To help you make your business successful. If you aren't successful then neither are they. This is a business about helping other people. The more people you help the bigger your business grows and the more successful you become.

Good network marketing businesses have great training programs. Providing you with all the skills and knowledge you need to build a successful business. They have a proven system which if followed will guarantee you success. With some of the better companies the training is provided free of charge. You just have to get yourself to the training sessions.

Earning potential is enormous and usually restricted only by your effort. There is the potential to become very wealthy from a network marketing business.

 So if you want to start your own business but don't know anything about running a business then network marketing is a great place to start.

If you would like more information about network marketing then email me at info@karennewton.co.uk or visit my website www.karennewton.co.uk and click on the appropriate link.

Property

This is one of my favourite investments despite how over regulated the industry is becoming.

Property offers leveraging, capital growth, income and tax benefits which is why it fits into most of the sections of my financial pyramid. So let's look at the benefits of having rental properties.

1. **Leveraging** – for a 15% deposit you can purchase a property using a buy to let mortgage. The mortgage is based on rental returns and not the amount of income you earn. The property becomes yours and provided the mortgage is paid each month remains yours. So if you were buying a property for £100,000 you would need a deposit of £15,000. A lender gives you the balance. You have

now turned £15,000 into a £100,000 income producing asset.

2. **Capital growth** – historically house prices double every 7 – 10 years. That doesn't mean they go up constantly as they don't but with the ups and downs they average a doubling in price over 7 – 10 years. Now, with today's economic problems you may doubt that but a couple of years ago I was in the car with my step-father. We drove past a house and he told me he had bought it for £2,000 and sold it for £4,000 and thought he had done very well at the time. When I got home I checked the price and found it up for sale at £269,000. Now step-father was 79 years old at the time. I don't know when he bought the property but if we assume he was 20 that is nearly 6 decades ago. Allowing for house prices to double every 10 years the value of the house would have been £4000 first decade, Decade 2

would be £8,000. Decade 3 would be £16,000. Decade 4 would be £32,000. Decade 5 the value would be £64,000 and in Decade 6 is would be £128,000. The house was £269,000 despite all the up's and downs, recessions and depressions over 60 years the house still more than doubled on average every 10 years.

3. **Income** - Property provides an income in the form of rents. Rents tend to move with economic times. As we earn more money through inflation then rents tend to go up. Although there is a mortgage to pay and other legal compliances you can still create a good income from rental property.   A 3 bedroom house in my area can currently be purchased for around £80,000. To purchase this with a 15% deposit you would need to have £12,000. Rents are currently around £550pcm. A mortgage for £68,000 at 4% would cost you around £230 per month in

repayments. Property Insurance costs around £10 per month and gas safety certificate is about £40 a year or about £3.30 a month. Rental income is £550 less total expenses of £243 profit would be £307 per month. Equivalent to £3684 per year. For a deposit of £12,000 you are earning a return on your money of just over 30%. (Remember in the section on compounding interest we were working on an average return of 14% which many people believe is not possible. Here we are making an average return of 30%)

4. **Tax Benefits** – Although property is an investment it is still run as a business and you can claim house expenses for running a business, your telephone costs and car expenses all as legitimate tax deductions. Other deductions include renovating the property and maintenance.

If you don't have the deposit to buy a property there are other options available giving you control of a property and the income that goes with it. This is covered in more detail through the mentoring program. Email info@karennewton.co.uk and put mentoring in the subject line if you would like more information on the mentoring program.

Deposits

For many people finding a deposit for the purchase of a property can be daunting. For my first property I used a gifted deposit. For other properties I have used a loan, credit cards, property equity and even sold personal items to raise the cash until the properties got to the stage of supporting themselves and generating sufficient income to give me the deposits I need to purchase other properties.

In the section on bad debt, I explained how credit cards used to purchase personal items were a bad debt but the cards could be used as good debt.

If you have sufficient credit on your cards you can drawdown the money and pay cash to purchase a property. This may seem unrealistic to you but let me give you an example. I have a credit line over several credit cards of £65,000. By using the money on those cards and cash that I have saved I can buy a property with no mortgage. I buy properties that need renovating. Once renovated the property should provide me with an extra 15,000 – 20,000 in capital value. I then put a mortgage on the property and use the mortgage money to pay off the credit cards. The surplus money goes towards the next purchase. – This is how you use credit cards for good debt but you must make sure you pay back the cards in full once you have the mortgage in place. If you don't then you could get yourself into worse debt.

Shares

Shares can provide an income through dividends and capital growth for a small regular investment.

In my book 'A beginner's guide to the Share Market' I explained the two strategies I use to invest in shares.

1. I invest for income by finding high yield dividend companies paying quarterly or 6 monthly dividends.
2. I invest for capital growth through buying undervalued companies and waiting for the value of the shares to go up. Once they have doubled in value I sell half the shares and reinvest the money in other shares.

There are many so called 'experts' who advocate that you must have £10,000 or more to start any investment in shares and then leave your investment for several years to get the benefit. For many who would like to invest in shares the thought of starting with £10,000 is unrealistic.

Throughout this book I advocate using small regular investments which over time through the theory of compounding interest allows even the smallest investor the opportunity to benefit from most investment opportunities. For me investing in shares is no different.

Investing a regular small amount of around £100 a month is a reasonable starting point. Companies like 'The Share Centre' allow you to deposit regular amounts from as little as £20 per month. With my 12 year old daughter we put £20 per week into a share trading account and once she has £100 she buys high yield dividend shares which are reinvested back into her portfolio. Having done this for a few years she is starting to build a good portfolio with a nice little income. Imagine what her portfolio will be worth when she is 20 years old or 30 years old or even 50 years old just by putting £20 per week into a share trading account.

This strategy is called 'pound cost averaging'. Shares go up in value as well as down on a daily basis. Buying shares, in one company, over a period of time allows you to ride out the highs and lows so over a year you get an average price paid per share. It may be that in month one the £100 investment will buy 100 shares at £1 per share. The following month those shares may have dropped to 50p a share and you can buy 200 shares for your £100 pound investment. The next month the shares may be worth £1.25 so you can only purchase 80 shares. If you average the cost over the three months you have purchased 380 shares costing you £300 so the average cost per share is 79p. This is just an example and doesn't allow for share trading fees or stamp duty.

If this type of investing is done through an ISA account or a SIPP then you have the benefit of tax free investing. It is easy to see through the use of an ISA or SIPP how investing over many years some people have managed to build portfolios over one million pounds in value.

Royalties

Royalties are another source of income. They are a commission paid to me for the sale of items to which I hold the rights.

This is the fifth book I have personally written and for which I receive royalties each time a book is purchased. For the time and effort spent writing I receive an income for the lifetime of the book. The lifetime being an unknown period of time it just depends on how popular the books are and how long they continue to sell for.

In addition to writing my own books, I hold licenses on books written by other people and these books also pay me a royalty when they sell. I can rebrand the books with my own cover design and make the books unique to me.

The third thing I do for Royalties is run a small publishing company which publishes other author's books. They get a royalty when the book sells and I also get a share of the royalty as the publisher of the books.

Royalties can be obtained from other sources not just books. Musicians are paid a royalty for every record they sell and for each time it is played on the radio. In the world of technology royalties are paid for software games and apps on mobile phones. In business you can be paid a royalty for an idea.

In the 1980's I was working in a bank in New Zealand. The bank was looking for a way to reduce its operating costs and asked its staff for ideas to save money. Several of the ideas were so simple but saved a lot of money. The bank paid a percentage of the savings to the staff member who came up with the idea. The staff member received a royalty for their idea for as long as it continued to provide the bank with a saving.

Do you have an idea for the next household gadget? Through the use of patents, trademarks and copyrights you can earn an income for the life of the product or idea.

Lending

Due to the economic crisis and banks no longer providing sufficient lending to meet the needs of individuals or businesses there has been an increase in online companies fulfilling this role. I'm not talking about loan sharks but FSA approved companies who get people like me to lend to people and business who need a loan. This is known as P2P (peer to peer) lending. Demand is currently far greater than the funds available.

As an individual you can lend as little as £10 up to a maximum of £25,000. You can make regular investments of whatever amount you want and once you have £10 in your account it is then loaned to a borrower. Your exposure is not to just one person limiting the risk of bad debt and losing your money. For example if a customer wants to borrow £100 then 10 different people would put £10 each towards making up the loan. You set the interest rates that you would like to receive. Currently I receive between 6.5% - 13% paid on a monthly basis. Loans are for 3 years or 5 years with the borrower able to repay at any time.

You can reinvest your money into more loans with the company and I have doubled my money over 18 months using the principals of compounding interest. Nice little set up and no administration work just sending my money online to the company each week through a standing order.

If you want to invest more than £25,000 then you need to become a business authorised through the FSA.

I hope this has given you an idea of some of the simple things you can do to improve income in your financial pyramid.

Once you have completed the 12 month mentoring program then we have more sophisticated types of investments available to improve your cashflow even more.

Growth

Under the growth section of the financial pyramid, I am looking for investments that will produce capital growth over a longer period of time. Some of the investments in this section are the same as investments used in other sections of the financial pyramid.

Property

As I have previously said this is one of my favourite investments, it fits into several sections of the financial pyramid.

We've already covered property in detail so this is just a quick recap. Property offers:

- Good leveraging – a small deposit normally around 15% will give your portfolio a capital injection as though you owned the whole property.
- Growth record – history shows us that despite the ups and downs over an average of 10 years property will double in value.
- An Island – Britain is an island and is unable to grow more land to build on. With a growing population there will always be demand for houses
- Income – rental property pays the cost of the mortgage and your legal obligations

and should leave you with some income for yourself.

- Tangible Asset – unlike other forms of investing such as shares and bonds where you only have a certificate for your money property is a tangible asset.

For more information on property please revisit the other chapters within this book.

Shares

When it comes to shares I invest for income and capital growth.

In the growth section I am looking at shares that are undervalued and I expect under normal trading conditions that the shares will increase in value.

I buy shares in companies new to the share market that are raising capital for exploration such as oil and gas companies and mining companies. In 2010 I bought shares in an oil exploration company. The shares doubled in value and I decided to sell the whole lot and get out as I thought for the results they were obtaining the price of the share was too high. A couple of days after I sold the shares they dropped quiet drastically in value. Way below what I thought the share price should be. I bought some more and they went up again and I sold them again. The shares are at a price level I would expect and as I don't see much in their future at present to justify the share going any higher I haven't bought any more but I still keep an eye on them just in case I see further opportunities.

Investing in these types of shares can be quite risky so I don't hold many. If you are looking at this type of investment then you really need to do your research thoroughly before taking the plunge and buying the shares.   I can tell you, I have had my fair share of losses along with my fair share of winners. A few months ago I bought into a company whose shares had dropped to 13p and had stayed there for a little while. I researched the company, I thought the company undervalued and bought shares in early trading in the morning. I then went about my normal business for the day.   When I checked back later in the afternoon the shares were down to 4p and I had lost considerable money.

If you go back to the picture of the financial pyramid you can see the higher we climb up the pyramid the riskier the investment becomes. If you can't afford to lose the money don't invest in the share market. Don't rush to start towards the top of the pyramid. Start at the bottom with slow steady progress allowing compounding interest to take effect is the best way to proceed.

Enterprise Investment Scheme (EIS)

The government has put in place a scheme (EIS) to encourage private investment in new business ventures. Occasionally, an opportunity comes my way and if I am satisfied with the venture then I will invest in the business.

I currently have shares in a company set up by a sportsman to raise the money he needed to get into his sport. The company was set up as he was unable to raise the sponsorship he needed.

As I write this a film company has approached me with a view to investing in a production they are putting together following the success of their previous films.

A simplified explanation of the EIS scheme is if you purchase shares in a company approved to participate in the EIS scheme and the company is successful then following certain criteria if you make a capital gains on your shares when they are sold then you are exempt from capital gains tax.

The company will advise you if they qualify for EIS investment. You will receive a certificate for any money you invest.

Angel Investing

This is where you provide a business with funding. You can be a mentor to the business or sit back and just receive a return on your investment. In this type of investing you need to be able to look closely at the accounts of a business and read between the lines. Make a decision on whether this business has the potential to grow and succeed or if it is faltering and looking for money to prop it up in which case I would walk away from the deal unless you were good at turning businesses around.

All types of businesses are looking for angel investing and investor expertise. With todays economic climate this is becoming more popular. I have seen businesses unable to get loans asking for investors to put up sums in excess of £5 million. The reasons they want the money can be to expand their business with new venues; raise capital to buy new machinery and provide mortgages for builders and investors.

You can get great returns and lose all your money. Caution is needed and investors should be experience before looking at this option.

Speculation

Speculation is the top tier of our financial pyramid and my advice is until you master all the other sections stay clear of this one.

Areas I consider as speculation are Spreadbetting, Forex and Futures. With a lot of knowledge, training and time many people etch a living from these areas but until you have built up your financial knowledge and wealth my advice is to stay clear of these types of investments.

Section 2 Summary

Section 2 has covered a lot of subjects through the use of my Financial Pyramid.

You have seen how having a business can provide massive tax advantages along with helping to build your income and net worth. Property offers some of the best leverage available to quickly build income and net worth.

There are many different types of investments and some will appeal to you and some won't. I hope this section has provided enough information to whet the appetite for further learning.

If you would like to be part of my mentoring program email me at info@karennewton.co.uk

Section 3

What we did and how we did it.

Section 3 – Introduction

When I have read investment books I have often been disappointed not to see more detail from the author on their particular investment and how they achieved their success. While some touch on their experience very few seem willing to provide actual details.

Throughout this book I have mentioned some of the investments that I hold and how I have achieved them but for you to truly understand how easy it can be to start on your journey I felt for credibility I needed to provide further detailed information.

Sometimes it is difficult to judge what is enough information and what is too much information and I hope I have managed to provide a balanced overview.

In providing more in depth information on my investments and business I hope to convey the simplicity of the actions rather than brag about the outcome. When I worked in banking I had a CEO who would often turn down new products because he felt they were too complicated. He always said 'banking is simple so keep it simple'.

I say to you, investing is simple so keep it simple. If it sounds complicated then stay away from it. Only invest in what you understand. Remember it was complicated banking which led to the credit crunch and the worst recession seen in a lifetime. It was complicated products that have continued to hold back world economies and stop world growth.

As you read my story please remember I am not writing it to brag but to show you how simple investing can be with financial education.

The Plan

In 1999 I wrote what became know as 'The Plan'. It was a simple statement that outlined what I wanted to achieve and how I was going to do it.

The Plan:

To achieve financial freedom and generate passive income from shares, rental properties, book royalties and business income.

The plan was written 12 years ago and still remains the same today. I think it will remain in place for many years to come.

Everyday I ask myself two questions. They are:

1. What have I done to improve my cashflow?
2. What have I done to improve my net worth?

I don't go to bed until I can honestly answer each of the above questions with a positive action.

Training

I am a strong believer in training. Throughout my life in whatever I've been doing when I felt I needed help to move to the next level I would get further training.

Training comes in different forms.

Formal Education – where I have attended night classes to get the qualifications I felt I needed at the time. During my time in New Zealand I studied at the local university Commercial Law, Business Management, Accounting and Quality Management. I have to admit for several years I felt like a professional student while building the knowledge I needed for the businesses I was running.

Training Courses – these are informal courses. Since returning to the UK I have attended weekend courses for Property Investing; Share Trading; Spreadbetting; Niche Marketing. And daytime courses for Network Marketing,

Property Investing and Share Trading. Often, the information provided is very specialised and well worth any time spent attending them. The cost sometimes puts people off attending which is a shame. I've attended free seminars and the information has allowed me to make thousands of pounds. I have attended expensive programs and walked away thinking what did I learn from that. Despite the varying results I would recommend where you can to attend seminars covering the topics of interest to you. You never know that may just be the seminar that makes you a millionaire.

Books – I love reading and in particular I buy investment and self-development books. I have so many books that one room in our house is now referred to as the library. The information I obtain from reading books will often send me in search of further information and further training courses. If you are taking the time to read this book then hopefully you also have the desire to improve you knowledge with further reading. For that reason I have enclosed at the back of the book a list of my favourite books and favourite authors.

DVD's/CD's - Listening to educational cd while driving the car is a way of utilising dead time. In fact, I find some of the exercises fun and a good way of breaking up a long drive. Tony Robbins has some great tapes on personal development which have been such fun to do that time on a trip of three or four hours has quickly flown by. It is surprising how much I remember from those exercises even though I was driving at the time.

The Wheel of Life

Both Paul J Meyer and Darren Hardy talk about the wheel of life and use this tool as part of their training.

The aim of the wheel of life is to ensure a balance between family, work, education, hobbies and spirituality. It is amazing how despondent someone becomes when the wheel is out of balance. It is also fun to work at getting the wheel to balance.

If you have read any of the programs by Paul J Meyer or Darren Hardy then you will understand what I am saying. If you've never come across it before check out Darren Hardy's website www.thecompoundeffect.com

Mentors

Earlier in the book I gave a list of people who have helped me as I have built businesses, investments and my Financial Education.

In addition to those people there are acquaintances with whom I get together on a regular basis to discuss ideas.

Sometimes working a business from home or investing can be a lonely life. So, I enjoy regular get together with other business owners and investors just to help keep me on the straight and narrow.

I also attend forums in my region for landlords and investors. I still attend seminars and workshops as there is still a lot for me to still learn. As my investment knowledge grows then I look for new investments and that involves more reading and more training. It's a cycle that help me increase my net worth and income.

Property

In June 2000 my husband & I had left New Zealand and moved to Australia with the intention of starting our investment business. We were in the country for a few days before returning to the UK following my mother's death. We had every intention of returning to Australia. Twelve days later my grandmother died then over the next eight months I lost six members of my family. Due to the amount of time my husband and I had spent at hospitals and funerals we decided to see what we could do with investments in the UK with a view to staying here for a longer term.

As we had only been in the country since June 2000 we had to wait until June 2001 to qualify for a mortgage to buy our first property. We started searching for a property in 2000. We found a property for sale around £54,000. We asked for a gifted deposit and the offer was declined. A month later the price had dropped to and we made another offer again asking for a gifted deposit and the offer was again turned down. A few months later the price of the property was again reduced in price. Again we put our offer in asking for a gifted deposit and this time the offer was accepted. We bought the property for £39,000. No money down deal. We borrowed £300 on a credit card to pay the solicitors fees. We moved into the property in June 2001.

The property had been empty for five years and needed a lot of work. The work was done over a few months and we obtained a home improvement loan for the renovations. We used the money to purchase our second property for cash at auction in September 2001.

In the meantime we finished the renovation work on the first property. The property was then revalued at £60,000 and we obtained an 85% mortgage.

When the second property was renovated we obtained a mortgage for 85% of the upgraded value. Between the two properties we managed to raise sufficient cash to repay the home improvement loan and the credit card. With the money leftover we were able to purchase two more below value properties.

And so the cycle continued, renovate the property, get the property revalued, remortgage up to 85% of the value and reinvest the money back into more properties.

We kept this simple system going until the problems with Northern Rock and the subsequent credit crunch. By this stage we had purchased 60 properties worth over £10 million pounds.

Since the credit crunch in 2008 borrowing money has become more difficult. It is still possible to follow the system we used to buy rental properties but it will take a longer period of time to build a portfolio. If you buy a property with cash quite a few lender require you to hold the property for 6 months before they will consider a mortgage due to the volatility in house prices.

There are lenders willing to lend for buy-to-let so it is still possible to build a property portfolio.

Shares

Since I was in my mid twenties I have owned shares in companies. During that time I've made a lot of money and lost a lot of money. I still continue to use a dual system of investing for high yield dividend and investing in small companies with a view to capital gains.

Where possible the investment is through Stocks & Shares ISA accounts. Where the shares do not qualify through ISA or I have used my full annual investment allowance I use an ordinary share trading account through my bank.

Successes and Failures

There are some people who will tell you how fantastic shares are and that they always make money. Don't believe them. No one knows what is going to effect the market and if it will go up or down. Unless you have a very sad life where you spend every minute of everyday sat in front of a computer watching every minute move, it is odds on that a movement will happen when you least expect it and that will make or lose you loads of money.

If you are going to invest in shares be prepared to lose money.

One of my greatest failures was during the 1987 share market crash. At the time I lived in New Zealand and had around $40,000 invested in shares. Britain and the US had crashed overnight and within 10 minutes of opening New Zealand did the same. I didn't even have chance to get through to the broker with a sell order (we didn't have online trading then) as his phone was engaged each time I rang. As I watched the price plummet I took the decision that I had already lost so much value in the first ten minutes of trading that I would hold on to the shares. I had shares in three companies and watched my holdings go from $40,000 in value to $5,000. Having decided to hold the shares I watched them slowly over the coming weeks and months start to climb in value back up to $20,000. It was at that time all 3 companies made the decision to privatise their companies and buy back their shares. I had no option but to sell at the price they offered and my total loss was $20,000.

There are however, some really good successes:

- Corus shares bought for 2p and sold at £4 profit £200,000
- TSB bought for £1 sold for £9 profit £27,000

I continue to invest money into shares each month. I maximise my ISA allowance, my husbands ISA allowance and when my daughter finally gets an ISA account we will also maximise her allowance. Any profits and capital gains made in these products are tax free. All dividends are reinvested back into shares.

I also have a bank share trading account and all surplus money from my investments that aren't used up through ISA goes into this trading account.

Commodities

Each month I purchase gold and silver bullion. This investment forms the basis of my financial pyramid. While this produces no income over the last decade there has been considerable capital gain. My preference is for gold ingots and American Eagle coins.

At this stage there is no plan to sell. I am keeping a watchful eye on Europe, Greece, Spain, Portugal, Italy and Ireland. If the euro collapses then I expect to see commodities increase substantially.

I am waiting for the day when I will be able to purchase a house with a few silver coins. That may seem extreme but as house prices go down, silver goes up.

Business

Throughout this book I have mentioned the importance of having a business. I have several businesses with more in the pipeline being developed. These businesses produce small but steady income on a monthly basis.

My current businesses are:

Rental Property Management – when you buy property as an investment it needs to be rented. I have used several companies and been disappointed with the service. Fees are high, service poor and when problems start everything gets given back for you to deal with the problem tenant. You are charged 6 monthly fees for resigning tenancies. I didn't like this so set up my own rental company. While the company is for my portfolio and my husband's portfolio we do manage properties for a few friends. When problems arise with the rentals, and they do sometimes occur, my company will handle all the legal work until tenants are evicted. We also do all the applications for CCJ's after the tenant has left.

Solar Panels - Although this business will not be up and running until 2012 I have included it here as it is now almost ready to begin trading. The government pays a feed-in-tariff for electricity generated from renewable energy. The solar panel business is to install solar panels on our rental properties allowing the business to receive the feed-in-tariff.

Publishing Company – I run a small publishing company originally set up to publish my books. The business has expanded to helping new authors get their first book published.

Niche Marketing - I produce products targeted to specific markets. These products are usually in the form of books, newsletters, dvd's and cd's. In addition to producing my own products the business holds licences to rebrand and sell other company's products.

Network Marketing – I joined a network marketing business to take advantage of another income stream available from the rental properties. The products offered by telecom plus are telephony and utilities. These are services needed in all homes.

P2P Lending – Peer to Peer lending has become popular since the 2008 credit crunch and banks failing to lend to individuals and businesses. P2P lending can be started initially as an investment through online companies. There is a restriction on the amount that can be lent. The current limit is £25,000. If you wish to lend more then you have to apply to the FSA for a licence and become a business not an investor.

Angel Investing – this little investment/business provides funding and expertise to businesses throughout the country. There is no restriction on the amount that can be invested into businesses.

Mentoring/Coaching — this little consultancy business helps like minded people set up and grow their own businesses and investments.

Section 3 – Summary

For the last decade Ron and I have planned, studied, found mentors and slowly put into practice what we have learned.

With no money to start our property investment we borrowed £300 on a credit card and turned it into £10 million in property. We used negotiation to get the deals we wanted; persistence in getting the right deals; knowledge gained from reading books like this one and attending seminars helped us put the deals together. We then had a dogged determination to make everything work for us. We had a vision for the type of lifestyle we wanted and set about building it.

Each investment and each business has been built slowly and steadily. We've started small with only a few pounds to get started and built from scratch each business and each investment. In some cases the £10 a week I started investing 11 years ago still continues today. Those investments have grown through compounding interest to such an extent that the £10 a week is no longer needed as they generate far more than that each week. It has become a habit rather than a need to keep the investment ticking over on a weekly basis.

Today when someone approaches me and says they have the perfect investment I just need to put £20,000 or more in to start it the answer is usually no. I still believe in starting small and testing the investment strategy to make sure it fits my formula for compounding interest and results.

Rather than buying existing businesses I still enjoy the challenge of building my own business from scratch. I still run my businesses from home. The space I have has just grown a little over the years. I started 11 years ago with a little computer desk and a personal computer crammed into the hallway of our first house. Today I have a large room in our home, a large desk and run the businesses from my laptop and mobile. The space has got larger, the equipment smaller, the businesses and investments bigger the time needed to run them less and less.

I believe business is turning full circle and the era of large corporations is being replaced by cottage industries -small businesses run from home producing millions of pounds in revenue each year.

In 2011 the National Statistics Office announced the growth in people becoming self-employed was at an all time high. This is a trend I like to think will continue for the foreseeable future.

There has never been a better time or a more urgent time to start building your own financial pyramid.

Section 4

Putting It All Together

How To Make £30,000+ A Month

How to make £30,000+ a month was the title for one of the first Niche Marketing products that I sold. Comprising of a book and a couple of cd's it explained how to set up a niche marketing business run from home. It proved to be a successful seller.

I've often wondered how many of the customers who purchased the product ever went on to build their businesses. So many people want to improve their lives but don't want to make the simple changes needed to make it happen. They buy books hoping it will provide the answers but usually fail to take the action needed to start the journey to financial freedom.

Throughout this book you will find simple steps which often need no action other than setting up a standing order from your bank and opening an investment account such as an ISA. Sadly, many will not take the 20 minutes maximum needed to do it. In 10 years time instead of building an income they will still be purchasing books like this and taking no action at all complaining that nothing works. Will you be one of them?

Most homes have computers and an internet connection so you have all the tools you need to get started.

Action Step 1

- Open an ISA account and set up a regular payment to it. Your own bank should have ISA accounts if you don't want to use them try a company like The Share Centre. While you learn about shares try using some of their recommendations. If you don't want to risk your money with a share isa open a cash isa.
- Open a P2P lending account and set up a regular payment to it. An online search

will provide you with plenty of names. The biggies in the industry are Zopa for residential lending and ThinCats for commercial lending. Set your interest rates and use the auto lend facility, that will ensure your money is relent as quick as possible and keeps working for you.

The maximum time spent setting up each of those investments should be no more than 20 minutes each. They will now continue for life or until you cancel them. With the P2P lending you will need to check the interest rates occasionally to ensure your money is being lent at the best possible rates, once a week should be enough.

If you've opened a stock and shares ISA it will need more monitoring and research to decide which stocks to buy. For best results look for high yield dividends companies usually found in the FTSE250. The share price for these companies tends to be less volatile than the FTSE100. Once you have your shares a weekly check should be sufficient to monitor progress.

With **Action Step 1** completed you have started your step towards earning £30,000+ a month. It won't happen over night as compounding interest needs time to work its magic. But it will happen.

Action Step 2

- Start a business. Any business of your choice. To reduce costs start as a sole trader.   Notify HMRC online that you have started and apply for a NIC exemption while you build your profits up to the minimum level at which it is compulsory to pay NIC contributions.

If you still haven't decided on the type of business to start then start a network marketing business. Contact me on info@karennewton.co.uk and let's get your business career underway. Network Marketing can be done on a part-time basis and for as little as 1 hour a week you can build a substantial business over a period of time. There is unlimited earning potential from a network marketing business.

Action Step 3

- Join my mentoring program by contacting me on info@karennewton.co.uk

You now have three simple action steps. If followed you can be earning £30,000+ a month. The length of time taken to be earning this income is up to you and the amount of time you are willing to commit to it. It might be 1 year from now, 5 years or 10 years. **It's your choice and you're decision.**

£30,000 is a starting point as once you've proved to yourself how easy it is to achieve then I am sure you will want to increase the amount even further.

What is your dream day?

Designing a new lifestyle can be daunting so how about designing your dream day?

From the time you wake up in the morning until you go to bed at night what would be your one perfect day?

I was asked this question when I work in a bank in New Zealand. The question was asked to help us get used to setting goals to help us achieve something outside of work to enable us to have a better balance in our lives.

I remember listening to people saying they wanted to lie in bed and not get up until lunchtime. Some wanted to take the day off and sit on the beach. Others wanted to go to an Allblack Rugby Match. As everyone in the room read out their perfect day I started to panic about announcing mine as it seemed so unrealistic compared to the others.

When it got to me I took a deep breath and read out my dream day. To spend the morning skiing in the Alps, pop into Monaco, have a long relaxing lunch followed by a little shopping or relaxing on the beach. Have dinner on a yacht before heading back to my place in the Alps.

As unrealistic as the perfect day seemed then it has become a bit more realistic today. I now have an apartment in the Alps and love nothing more than being in the snow first thing in the morning. Having a long lunch in the local restaurants and heading off to the shops later in the day. Monaco is 7 hours drive away so I'm still working on how to fit shopping and dinner on a yacht in and get back to my apartment in one day. But the secret here is I am still working on my perfect day.

So I ask the question again. What is your perfect day? What are you doing to make it happen?

What Next?

I hope you have gained some ideas from reading this book. The financial world as we know it is changing and changing very quickly. Nobody knows if the euro will survive but if you are better prepared financially you will be in a good place to survive 2012 and all that comes in the aftermath.

Good luck on your financial journey.

I always enjoy reading about your successes so feel free to email me at
info@karennewton.co.uk

Thank you for reading this book.

Recommended Reading

Rich Dad, Poor Dad – Robert Kiyosaki

Cashflow Quadrant – Robert Kiyosaki

Rich Dad's Guide to Investing – Robert Kiyosaki

Rich Dad Prophecy – Robert Kiyosaki

Increase Your Financial IQ – Robert Kiyosaki

Who took my money – Robert Kiyosaki

Guide to Becoming Rich – Robert Kiyosaki

The Business School – Robert Kiyosaki

Conspiracy of the Rich – Robert Kiyosaki

Unfair Advantage – Robert Kiyosaki

The Real Book of Real Estate – Robert Kiyosaki

Guide to Investing in Gold & Silver – Michael Maloney

Real Estate Riches – Dolf de Roos

Making Money Made Simple – Noel Whittaker and Roger Moses

Making More Money – Noel Whittaker and Roger Moses

Living Well In Retirement – Noel Whittaker and Roger Moses

High Powered Investing for Dummies – various authors

The Richest Man in Babylon – George S Clason

Think and Grow Rich – Napoleon Hill

Feel The Fear and Do It Anyway – Susan Jefferies

Liquid Millionaire – Stephen Sutherland

Instant Cashflow – Bradley J Sugars

Buffettology – Mary Buffett and David Clark

The New Buffettology – Mary Buffett and David Clark

You, Property and Your Pension – Ajay Ahuja

The Buy-to-let Bible – Ajay Ahuja

Naked Trader – Robbie Burns

Naked Trader 2 – Robbie Burns

Naked Trader 3 – Robbie Burns

How to Make Money In Stocks – William J O'Neill

The Commodities Investor – Phillip Scott

Free Capital – Guy Thomas

The Money Gym – Nicola Cairncross

Secrets of the Millionaire Mind – T Harv Eker

The Compound Effect – Darren Hardy

Focal Point – Brian Tracy

Make A Living From Property – Karen Newton

Beginners Guide to the Share market – Karen Newton

29 Hours A Day – Karen Newton

Insiders Guide to Investing In Art – Karen
Newton

Make A Living From Property

From June 2001 until September 2007 Karen used £300 borrowed on a credit card and turned it into a £10 million property portfolio.

Make A Living From Property is a step-by-step guide showing you how you can do the same.

The book is out of general print but can be bought as a digital version direct from Karen by emailing info@karennewton.co.uk or visit the website www.karennewton.co.uk

**Beginners Guide
To The
Sharemarket**

*A beginner's guide
to the sharemarket is a simple step
by step to investing in shares.*

*Karen explains her two strategies of
investing for high yield dividends and
capital growth through undervalued
companies or penny share
companies.*

*Understand the power of compound
interest through the story of the fairy
godmother and the magic train and*

you will think twice about how simple it really is to acquire great wealth.

This book is out of general print but available in a digital version. For further information email info@karennewton.co.uk or visit the website www.karennewton.co.uk

29 Hours A Day

Have you ever wondered why some people seem to do so much during the day while you struggle with your workload.

29 hours a day shows you simple techniques to improve your time management skills and achieve more in a day than you thought possible.

This book is out of general print but is available in a digital version. For further information email info@karennewton.co.uk or visit the website www.karennewton.co.uk

Insider Guide to Investing in Art

Rembrandt, Monet and Picasso are some of the worlds best know artists. Today their paintings are worth millions. Yet, they started their careers with little or no money needing supporters to help them survive from day to day.

Insider Guide to Investing in Art will help you identify the artists of today who are likely to be the successes of tomorrow. Buy their art today and it could be worth millions tomorrow.

This book is out of general print but available in a digital version. For further information email _info@karennewton.co.uk_ or visit the website _www.karennewton.co.uk_

Insiders Guide to Investing in Art

Karen Newton

Coming in 2012

Due for release in late 2012, Karen's new book is a guide to Niche Marketing. It covers how to identify niche markets, creating your own unique products and selling them and building a successful business.

www.ingramcontent.com/pod-product-compliance
Lightning Source LLC
Chambersburg PA
CBHW051445170526
45166CB00001B/123

9781477659953